TOLKIEN'S

Ordinary Virtues

Exploring the
Spiritual Themes of
The Lord of the Rings

MARK EDDY SMITH

InterVarsity Press
Downers Grove, Illinois

InterVarsity Press
P.O. Box 1400, Downers Grove, IL 60515-1426
World Wide Web: www.ivpress.com
E-mail: mail@ivpress.com

InterVarsity Press® is the book-publishing division of InterVarsity Christian Fellowship/ USA®, a student movement active on campus at hundreds of universities, colleges and schools of nursing in the United States of America, and a member movement of the International Fellowship of Evangelical Students. For information about local and regional activities, write Public Relations Dept., InterVarsity Christian Fellowship/USA, 6400 Schroeder Rd., P.O. Box 7895, Madison, WI 53707-7895, or visit the IVCF website at <www.ivcf.org>.

Scripture quotations, unless otherwise noted, are from the New Revised Standard Version of the Bible, copyright 1989 by the Division of Christian Education of the National Council of the Churches of Christ in the USA. Used by permission. All rights reserved.

Cover and interior illustrations: Jack Stockman
ISBN 0-8308-2312-3
Printed in the United States of America ∞

Library of Congress Cataloging-in-Publication Data

Smith, Mark Eddy, 1967-
  Tolkien's ordinary virtues: exploring the spiritual themes of The lord of the rings/ Mark Eddy Smith.
    p. cm.
  ISBN 0-8308-2312-3 (alk. paper)
  1. Tolkien, J. R. R. (John Ronald Reuel), 1892-1973. Lord of the rings. 2. Tolkien, J. R. R. (John Ronald Reuel), 1892-1973—Religion. 3. Christianity and literature—England—History—20th century. 4. Christian fiction, English—History and criticism. 5. Fantasy fiction, English—History and criticism. 6. Middle Earth (Imaginary place) 7. Spiritual life in literature. 8. Virtue in literature. I. Title.
  PR6039.O32 L637 2002
  823'.912—dc21   2001051569

18	17	16	15	14	13	12	11	10	9	8	7	6	5	4	3	2
16	15	14	13	12	11	10	09	08	07	06	05	04	03	02		

In loving memory of
my great aunt,
Marion Edith Smith,
who gave me my first copy of
The Lord of the Rings
in 1978, as a birthday present.

Contents

Part Three A NEW BEGINNING

Part Four HELP UNLOOKED-FOR

Part Five THE GOOD FIGHT

Part Six THE ROAD GOES EVER ON AND ON

Acknowledgments

The author wishes to gratefully acknowledge the following for their invaluable support:

Cindy for being wise enough to suggest the project and foolish enough to trust me with it, and for being a great editor; Ruth for her stewardship not only of the planet but of our friendship and my book; Mom and Dad for their love and faith; Beth and Charlie for their love and celebration; Cheryl for imparting some of her courage to me when I needed it most; Kathy for a wonderful cover; Anne for her justice and mercy in regard to my schedule; Andy for his encouragement and perspective; Randy for his trustworthiness as a checker of accuracy; Eirik for sharing his wisdom when mine faltered; Margaret for always hoping for me; Bobbie and Joe for their generosity; Andrew and Sally for their hospitality; the IVP community for their friendship and mirth; the Tolkien reading group for sharing the love and persevering; the Ring at Rez for their imagination and exuberance; the Wheaton in England group for a thousand examples of providence; Staci and Andrew for forgiving my failure to reach page 247; the Father, Son and Holy Spirit for authoring all virtues; and of course J. R. R. Tolkien for simply taking a lifetime to explore Middle-earth.

In spite of the best efforts of all these wonderful people, this book is incomplete and imperfect, and for that the author in all humility accepts full responsibility.

Introduction

The Lord of the Rings!

Frodo Baggins, at the council of Elrond, saying, "I will take the Ring, though I do not know the way."

Gandalf the Grey sliding into the abyss, crying, "Fly, you fools!"

Sam Gamgee, a gardener from the Shire, "turning into a creature of stone and steel, which neither weariness, nor despair, nor endless, barren miles could subdue."

The mere recollection of these phrases can move me to tears. I have been reading this tale since I was eleven years old, taking it from my shelf every year or so and returning to Middle-earth, drinking its virtues, pulling sustenance from it the way a tree draws earth with its roots. I never grow weary of it. As I get older and learn more of what sort of person I am and continue sojourning in the rich soil of the Shire and the high tower of Minas

Tirith, I discover that many of my notions of what is good and right and noble in this world have their source in that one.

Visiting Middle-earth is like returning home, a blessing made all the more poignant the farther I feel from my real one. Some of my oldest friends live there, and I learn more about them every time we meet. Some, like Sam, are simple and accessible, and yet their deeds are awe-inspiring. Others, like Tom Bombadil or Tree-beard, only grow more mysterious and inscrutable. It is a vast, carefully detailed world, wondrous evidence of the capacity for imagination with which our Creator has endowed us. Tolkien delights in describing every flower and every stand of trees, every curve of the river and every turn of the trail. His delight is so infectious that whenever I am hiking through some corner of this world that is still worthy to be called "unspoiled," much of what I see and hear and smell reminds me of Ithilien, Lothlórien or the Shire, as if I had actually been there and was now returning.

In Middle-earth I have found a training ground, a place where I can apprentice to those whose gifts of charity, wisdom, kind-ness, mercy, love and faithfulness far surpass my own. Soon after reading *The Lord of the Rings* for the first time, I was in a Sunday school class in which we read a section of the Old Testament. I made the observation that it sounded a lot like Tolkien. My Sun-day school teacher gently corrected me. "No, Mark," she said, "Tolkien sounds a lot like the Bible."

This is not incidental. Tolkien was a devout Catholic from early childhood. He believed that his history of Middle-earth was on some level essentially true, that he was not so much inventing it as discovering it. I am not suggesting it was inspired in the biblical sense of the word, but I do believe that God had a hand in writing it, working through the circumstances of Tolkien's life, speaking to him through his intuition, endowing him with wisdom to understand the intricacies of the plot of the ongoing story called Creation.

C. S. Lewis credited a late-night conversation with Tolkien and another friend as being the crux of his conversion from a guarded theism to an enthusiastic Christianity. The essential insight he gained from them was that myths are not by definition lies. The story of Christ is a "true myth, a myth that works on us in the same way as the others, but a myth that *really happened.*" Part of Tolkien's argument went like this:

> We have come from God, and inevitably the myths woven by us, though they contain error, will also reflect a splintered fragment of the true light, the eternal truth that is with God. Indeed, only by myth-making, only by becoming a "sub-creator" and inventing stories, can Man aspire to the state of perfection that he knew before the Fall. Our myths may be misguided, but they steer however shakily towards the true harbour. (reconstructed by Humphrey Carpenter in *J. R. R. Tolkien,* p. 151)

Tolkien never preaches. He is not offering a sermon but telling a story. He gives the characters freedom to take on a life of their own, to make their own decisions as it were. He hated allegory of any kind but made a distinction between allegory and applicability. In his foreword to the Ballantine paperback edition (I use the

ninety-fifth printing for references throughout, with occasional
references to the eleventh printing of *The Silmarillion,* citing
volume number and page) he writes, "The one resides in the
freedom of the reader, and the other in the purposed domination
of the author."

Here then is my humble attempt at searching out some of the
applicabilities of *The Lord of the Rings.* Middle-earth is so self-
contained, so fully and minutely realized, and yet at the same
time so removed from what we fondly refer to as the real world,
that we may learn more easily from it than by studying the con-
voluted facts of our own history. Along with *The Silmarillion,*
which details the cosmology, mythology and tragedy leading up
to the War of the Rings (as well as volumes of Lost and Unfinished Tales), we can see the beginning, the middle and the end—
a complete story. Again, Tolkien's work copies the Bible in this
large scope. While it can never supplant the Bible, it may do its
part to supplement it, so that we see again, from a different perspective, the same essential and eternal truths.

Part One

ORDINARY VIRTUES

Book I in *The Fellowship of the Ring*

1

SIMPLICITY

HOBBITS ARE A RUSTIC PEOPLE, with little use for machinery and little concern for the affairs of the larger world. They are fond of eating (plenty and often), and they prize predictability over originality. They despise adventures of any kind, considering them (rightly), 'nasty, disturbing, uncomfortable things. Make you late for dinner!'" (*The Hobbit,* p. 18). Hobbits are unlikely heroes.

Nevertheless, no less august a person than Gandalf the Grey, a wizard of some renown, chose a hobbit, Mr. Bilbo Baggins, as chief burglar for a group of Dwarves seeking to reclaim their ancestral home from a fearsome dragon. His choice seemed the height of foolishness to the Dwarves, but in the end they discovered that cleverness, resourcefulness and leadership may sometimes be found in the most unlikely places, and indeed they almost surely would not have succeeded in the adventure without their burglar's assistance.

Gandalf apparently had some inkling of Bilbo's potential, but he probably had no idea of the consequences of his choice. That Bilbo would find the One Ring, lost for generations, that he would play a part in the greatest conflict of the Third Age of Middle-earth, was surely beyond the wildest dreams of any of the wise, and it did not come into any of the old prophecies. What seemed little more than a mad whim, an amusing footnote in the annals of history, became the seed of something that would shake the tower of Barad-dûr, ancient fortress of the Dark Lord Sauron.

Nothing in the long, uneventful history of the Shire suggested that its inhabitants might be capable of wielding such power. Centuries of peace had made Hobbits soft. Yet they had not lost the strength with which they were created. "There is a seed of courage hidden (often deeply, it is true) in the heart of the fattest and most timid hobbit, waiting for some final and desperate danger to make it grow" (I:178).

It is the nature of seeds to lie dormant as long as necessary. And once they have sprouted, they need time and careful tending in order to grow. Simple people can be maddeningly short-sighted and provincial, but the cost of gaining wisdom and perspective is often calamity. As Frodo says, contemplating his departure:

> I should like to save the Shire, if I could—though there have
> been times when I thought the inhabitants too dull and stupid
> for words, and have felt that an earthquake or an invasion of

dragons might be good for them. But I don't feel like that now. I feel that as long as the Shire lies behind, safe and comfortable, I shall find wandering more bearable: I shall know that somewhere there is a firm foothold, even if my feet cannot stand there again. (I:88-89)

An example of Hobbits' maddening simplicity comes in the Birthday Party that opens the tale. All the Bracegirdles, Hornblowers, Proudfoots and other clans gather, not so much to honor Bilbo as to take advantage of the opportunity of feasting for free, enjoying spectacular fireworks and enduring the inevitable Speech. They do not understand, nor do they care to learn, the part that Bilbo played in defeating a dragon or in bringing about peace between Dwarves, Wood-elves and the Men of the Lake. Few in the Shire even believe his tales; they think him eccentric at best and completely cracked at worst. It is hard to be patient with such folk.

Strength is not created by adversity; it is merely awakened by it. The hobbits are defended on many fronts by more sophisticated people who do not believe that simplicity is a sign of weakness. As Aragorn says at Elrond's Council, "If simple folk are free from care and fear, simple they will be" (I:299). But this protection does not diminish the possibility that the most heroic deeds may be accomplished, or at least attempted, by the very same simple folk that are thus sheltered.

Before all is said and done, the hobbits shall have their calamity, and all of them will have the chance to learn of what stuff they are made, for wisdom and perspective are more important than safety. But that comes later. In the meantime they have to be protected from "foes that would freeze their hearts" (I:299) long enough to confront a more Hobbit-sized disaster. It is to be hoped that even after their day of reckoning they will continue to be a simple people, only wiser and more compassionate. Indeed, throughout the adventures of the three hobbits who accompany Frodo, they call upon their plain Hobbit-sense in their darkest moments and find that it sustains them.

On the other hand, there is often more to the simplest of our friends than it appears. Even Frodo is surprised by Sam's pensive and poetic response to the Elves they meet as they are leaving Hobbiton.

> "They are quite different from what I expected—so old and young, and so gay and sad, as it were." Frodo looked at Sam rather startled, half expecting to see some outward sign of the odd change that seemed to have come over him. It did not sound like the voice of the old Sam Gamgee that he thought he knew, but it looked like the old Sam Gamgee sitting there, except that his face was unusually thoughtful. (I:117-18)

It is all too easy to fall into patterns of relationship wherein all responses are predictable because we ourselves are saying nothing new. It often requires seeing friends in different contexts, in the company of strangers, to open our eyes to the unsuspected depths of their character.

If simplicity is a virtue, then living simple lives and cherishing simple pleasures are all that is required for our lives to have value. We need not feel guilty when we suspect we should be doing more for God's kingdom, for when he needs us he will call us, and until then we can be content to husband our strength, put down roots and enjoy the good things that have been given us. This is not to say that we shouldn't seek to improve ourselves or minister to those around us, only that limiting our efforts to our immediate family and neighbors is sufficient until our calling has been revealed.

When God does call us, it may be to a journey of danger and terror, with the possibility of no return, or it may be to the simpler danger and terror of confronting a boss whose practices seem a little shaky. The most simple among us are not safe from these possibilities. On the other hand, it may be that our calling is simply to live well in the midst of the community we were born in. This is not to be despised. The tale of Frodo and his friends may give us hope that we will be given the strength and the help we need to accomplish whatever task is set before us.

II

GENEROSITY

HE LORD OF THE RINGS BEGINS, as I mentioned earlier, with a Birthday Party. Although the real action of the story, wherein Frodo and his friends leave the Shire, does not begin till twelve years later, this is an appropriate place to start. Birthdays and the giving and receiving of presents have a strange significance in the history of the Ring. Gollum, who held the Ring for many years before Bilbo came upon it, maintained that it had been a birthday present from his grandmother, "who had lots of beautiful things of that kind" (I:82). In truth, while it was indeed his birthday when his friend Déagol found the Ring in the river, Gollum, then called Sméagol, murdered Déagol to claim it.

Bilbo himself maintained, to all but a few close friends, that for his part he had won the Ring from Gollum in a riddle contest.

The riddle contest did take place, but he had put his hand on the Ring in the dark before he met Gollum. By claiming to have won it, he wished to ease his conscience of the charge that he had stolen it, as from Gollum's point of view he certainly had. No one in the history of the Ring had ever given it to another voluntarily.

Now, a curious reversal is to be found in the traditions of Hobbit birthday parties. Presents, rather than being given to the one having a birthday, are instead given by the guest(s) of honor to all who attend the party. Many of these gifts are merely recycled "mathoms" which get passed throughout the Shire, but this upside-down tradition paves the way for a unique transaction that begins to break the cycle of destruction wrought by the Ring.

Preparing to leave the Shire, Bilbo gives away the greater part of his belongings, taking with him only "a few oddments" (I:55). He has always been generous with his money and has "many devoted admirers among the hobbits of poor and unimportant families" (I:41). On this occasion he invites everyone who lives nearby (and quite a few who live far away) and gives away extraordinary gifts, far beyond what custom dictates. In addition he gives away most of his household goods with notes attached to various members of the community, some with jokes or pointed barbs, but most to hobbits in genuine need. Partly this effulgence of generosity is intended to allow Bilbo to leave the Shire unencumbered by many belongings, but in the main it serves to build momentum for giving away the one thing he can't bear to part with: the Ring.

In the end the gift giving doesn't really help, but with Gandalf's

assistance Bilbo is finally able to pass on the Ring to Frodo and
be rid of it once and for all. It is an extraordinary achievement.
In this single act not only does he break the cycle of murder and
lies that surrounds the Ring, but in so doing he sets a precedent
that may eventually allow the Ring to be destroyed. And on a
more personal level, it allows him to leave behind his beloved
Shire not only unencumbered but actually free.

Frodo, in turn, receives the Ring freely, and though it grows
on his mind in much the same way that it grew on Bilbo's, he
does not have to deal with any guilt concerning the manner of
his obtaining it. In the end this will help him not at all to release
it, any more than Bilbo's scheme of giving away everything at
once helps him. Yet without that initial innocence and freedom it
is unlikely that Frodo would have gotten very far. A guilty conscience gnaws at the soul, as Sméagol found in dealing with the
murder of his friend. Doubt is cast upon one's ability to do anything right or pure, and despair knocks all the more insistently.
Freedom from this is the gift that Bilbo gives to his heir, at the
same time that he is saddling him with a nearly unbearable burden.

Generosity is not wholly about giving away possessions. Those
that have little in the way of material wealth may still be generous, if only in their opinions and in the report that they give to
others. When the old Gaffer, Sam Gamgee's father, is holding
forth at the Ivy Bush Inn, he informs all present that "a very
nice, well-spoken gentlehobbit is Mr. Bilbo, as I've always said"
(I:42). When the story of Frodo's parents' boating accident
comes up, he responds to the rumor of a tussle by saying, "There

isn't no call to go talking of pushing and pulling. Boats are quite tricky enough for those that sit still and look no further for the cause of trouble" (I:43). Generosity of this type is a wonderful defense against gossip; it is a sign, what's more, of trustworthy character.

On the other hand, the influence of an evil ring is not required for virtues to become twisted. The notorious Sackville-Bagginses, cousins of Bilbo and next in line to inherit his household before Frodo was adopted, fervently believe that they deserve Bag End, though they had no part in its building. In such ways Hobbits are very human (if I can be forgiven for using the term). They are not pure, sinless creatures, innocent victims of an evil too big for them, but a fallen people, much like ourselves, who have to choose whether they will be generous and kindly or petty and mean-spirited.

When we can give out of our abundance, freely and without resentment, and when we can receive gifts from others with neither guilt nor a sense of entitlement, then we can be free of all our possessions, and they will have no hold over us. Generosity does not always seem a grand virtue, but it is often one of the most difficult. As Jesus said, "It is easier for a camel to go through the eye of a needle than for someone who is rich to enter the kingdom of God" (Matthew 19:24).

"For mortals it is impossible, but for God all things are possible" (Matthew 19:26).

III

FRIENDSHIP

THERE IS NO GREATER TREASURE in Middle-earth (or anywhere else for that matter) than friends. For all the benefits of being unencumbered, Frodo is fortunate to find he has several such treasures and that three of them refuse to be left behind.

Merry, Pippin and Sam are not perfect friends. They poke their noses into Frodo's personal affairs; they spy on him, scheme behind his back and entirely fail to abide by his wishes. "My dear old hobbit, you don't allow for the inquisitiveness of friends," says Merry (I:137) when their conspiracy is unmasked. To Frodo's amazement, they know all about his decision to leave the Shire and even about the Ring. They are, however, resolved to guard his secrets more closely than he has himself. They are better than perfect; they are true.

Friendship alone has little strength to overcome evil. The four hobbits are easily lulled by Old Man Willow and later again by the Barrow Wight. They remain hidden from the Black Riders mainly by luck, and without the intervention of Tom Bombadil and the Elves they might never have made it to Bree. Throughout the adventure the main benefit of their friendship is simply that they get to enjoy each other's company, to laugh and sing together, and to comfort and encourage each other. They cannot fight Black Riders, they have less knowledge of the lands outside the Shire than Frodo does, and they have no overarching wisdom to guide him. Nevertheless, even the Elves (who hate to give advice) urge him to take such friends as he can trust.

Frodo has a hard time accepting his friends' devotion. The reasons for this are hinted at but never explicitly stated. For one thing, his own sense of loyalty urges him to protect his friends by leaving them behind. But also, as an orphan, he has a profound fear of being abandoned—and if even Bilbo has left him, how can he trust these other friends? The Ring Frodo has carried for twelve years has surely had its effects, taking his sense of loss and amplifying it, whispering to him that there is no end to losing. Finally, and in a certain sense rightly, he does not consider himself worthy of such friends as would die for him.

But in spite of all this, and maybe even because of it, when Frodo's own loyalty is tested he chooses not to abandon his friends. When he and his companions are captured and buried in the Barrow Downs, and the wight is chanting a spell to hold them forever underground, Frodo has a sudden vision: he could slip on the Ring and escape alone, to run free upon the grass. He would grieve his friends yet comfort himself that there was nothing else he could have done. No one would blame him for leaving them behind in that impossible situation. But then he would be as faithless as he fears his friends could be. The seed of courage buried deep in Hobbits opens up inside him then, and he calls out to Tom Bombadil.

They are all rescued, of course, but Frodo does not thereby lose his sense of doom. At every stage he is unwilling to allow his dearest friends to share in his peril. The Ring may be whispering that only one hand can wield it and that their loyalty is offered only in the hope that they might have a claim to it themselves. But in order for the quest to succeed, Frodo will, before the end, be required to learn the true nature of friendship and the importance of receiving it, trusting in it and leaning on it when his own considerable strength gives way.

When the hobbits finally reach Bree, they are confronted with an outsider who asks leave to join their Company. He is a rascally looking fellow, but another aspect of the Ring's influence on Frodo is that he can perceive things that others cannot. He understands implicitly that "all that is gold does not glitter" (I:212). Based on this perception he accepts Strider, little understanding who he truly is.

He is Aragorn, the chief of a band of Rangers whose self-appointed task is to protect the lands round about the Shire from trolls and wolves and other evils. He offers his services as a guide, but he expects something in return. He has the look of a rogue, but he is not after any money they might have. He has roamed on the fringes of civilization for many long years, and his job has been thankless, yet he does not desire gratitude. He has long hidden his true identity as an heir of kings, but he does not wish for recognition. He has been lonely and misunderstood, and what he craves above all is simply friendship. The more the hobbits get to know this mysterious Ranger, the more remarkable does this fact become.

The friendship of Gandalf is equally remarkable. Although he is accounted mighty even by the strong, he never considers anyone beneath his notice or care. Indeed it is Gandalf's friendship that allows him to convince Bilbo to relinquish the Ring. Although he reveals a tiny portion of his power, looming over the hobbit threateningly, that is not the turning point; and had he not been Bilbo's friend, the move might have been disastrous, pushing Bilbo to use the Ring and escape. In the end Gandalf diminishes himself and says, "I wish you would trust me, as you used" (I:56). Only then does Bilbo relent.

"Many proclaim themselves loyal, / but who can find one worthy of trust?" (Proverbs 20:6). Most of us wish to be loyal to our friends but find it a difficult virtue in practice. When friendship gets in the way of our own aspirations, it is easy to find reasons for stopping short of a full commitment. It requires a servant's heart, like Sam's, to lay aside our plans, simple as they may be, and follow a friend into danger and exile, but that is precisely what true friends do.

IV

HOSPITALITY

HE BIBLE ENCOURAGES US to show hospitality to strangers, "for by doing that some have entertained angels without knowing it" (Hebrews 13:2). Fatty Bolger has no wish to share in Frodo's perils, but he still wishes to do his part, which is to prepare a house for Frodo, knowing he will not stay there long, and to host the companions before they leave. Then he has the more difficult task of keeping up the pretense that Frodo continues to dwell there and of awaiting the Black Riders who will inevitably track the hobbit party as far as that house. This simple gift is not so high or noble as Merry, Pippin and Sam's, but it is essential to the mission's initial success and requires someone trustworthy.

Farmer Maggot knows nothing of the Ring. He is not even, strictly speaking, a friend, except to Merry, who has not yet joined Frodo and the others. All Maggot knows is that a Black Rider has ridden down his lane and asked for Baggins. A lesser hobbit might shut out Frodo and his friends the moment he hears them give the same name, for fear of what he is getting himself into, but not Maggot. Though he distrusts those from Hobbiton, being from the Marish himself, he recognizes Pippin and calls off his dogs. Then not only does he offer Frodo's party dinner and beer, but he puts himself in danger by driving them to the ferry under cover of darkness.

Farmer Maggot does not ask, in return, to be told what the commotion is about. "I am not asking you to tell me anything you have a mind to keep to yourself; but I see you are in some kind of trouble. Perhaps you are thinking it won't be too easy to get to the Ferry without being caught?" (I:127). His stoutheartedness is a great encouragement to the trio (as is his beer), and his is a wonderful example of someone taking responsibility for their land and those who travel over it. Later they will learn that he is a friend of Tom Bombadil, but even that knowledge can hardly raise him any higher in their esteem.

The discernment and discretion of hosts can go a long way toward putting guests at ease. Respecting privacy and not passing judgment, not offering unsolicited advice, can bless the weary traveler as much as food and warmth and company. It's part of the "expecting nothing in return" that is the mark of the most generous hosts. We do not need to fear those we take into our homes, that they might be wicked or uncouth. "But love your enemies, do good, and lend, expecting nothing in return. Your reward will be great, and you will be children of the Most High;

for he is kind to the ungrateful and the wicked" (Luke 6:35). It is difficult to distinguish between the fair and the foul, and it is better to risk being taken advantage of by rogues than to miss an opportunity to minister to those in desperate need.

Tom Bombadil is a considerably more formidable host than Farmer Maggot. He is older than the trees, known by many names, stronger than wight or willow, and even the Ring has no power over him. He can wear it and remain opaque, or watch Frodo put it on and not lose sight of him. He knows many tales, both merry and sad, and has a great store of wisdom and love for the simple life he has chosen for himself, for the trees and the animals, and for Goldberry. He rescues the hobbits when they need rescuing, he feeds and rests them when they are hungry and weary, and he entertains them when they are feeling bored. But for all his ridiculous power, the only thing he offers them is no more than what Farmer Maggot did: hospitality and safe passage through his land.

For Barliman Butterbur, proprietor of the Prancing Pony, providing hospitality to strangers is a business. Thus he is hospitable with somewhat less generosity than those of amateur status. He is too busy to give his full attention to anybody, and so he has never really gotten to know Strider, though he has often hosted him. He has forgotten to send Gandalf's letter on to Hobbiton and almost forgets to give it to Frodo when he arrives. Nevertheless, Butterbur does what he can for the companions. When he is told that the Black Riders come from Mordor, he quails. Frodo asks, "Are you still willing to help me?"

He replies, "I am. More than ever. Though I don't know what

the likes of me can do against, against—"

His words falter, but Strider finishes the sentence for him.
"Against the Shadow in the East. Not much, Barliman, but every
little bit helps. You can let Mr. Underhill stay here tonight, as Mr.
Underhill, and you can forget the name of Baggins, till he is far
away" (I:210-11). This he does, and the hobbits survive another
night.

If nothing else, hospitality provides weary travelers with rest.
Throughout the journey, at times and places unlooked for, the
hospitality of strangers succors the friends and allows them a
chance to spend a night or two in peace, so that their wayfaring
is not simply hardship and danger unabated. No journey of any
moment can be attempted without occasions of rest, as we would
do well to remember, should we ever have occasion to undertake
one.

V

FAITH

HENEVER FRODO AND HIS FRIENDS come into danger, the best they can do is call for help. When their efforts to free Merry and Pippin from the Great Willow fail, and it threatens to kill them, Frodo finds himself running about crying, "Help! Help! Help!" (I:154). He is answered by Tom Bombadil, the only one in the Old Forest with the power to help them.

Frodo calls upon Tom again in the Barrow and is again answered. Indeed whenever he calls for unseen help, he is answered. When the Black Riders assail the hobbits at the foot of Weathertop, long before Frodo develops the strength of will to resist their call to put on the Ring, he simply throws himself to the ground and cries aloud, "O Elbereth, Gilthoniel!" (I:240).

According to *The Silmarillion,* Elbereth is the Elvish name for

Varda, who was created by Eru, the One, and who in her turn created the stars. She is one of the Valar, angelic beings who dwell in Middle-earth and take part in its creation. Her name is more deadly to the Ringwraiths than Frodo's feeble knife swipe. For Frodo has been thrust into a story whose beginnings predate Middle-earth itself, and there are powers only dimly glimpsed by the oldest and wisest in Middle-earth, powers that are concerned to help Frodo finish his task. Though he knows but little of these beings, their history or their nature, Frodo hears himself on many occasions calling upon their names. It is an awesome thing that they answer.

We are surrounded by powers that we cannot see, and not all of them are evil. Elisha, a prophet of ancient Israel, asks that the army of God be revealed to his attendant, and the servant sees that "the mountain was full of horses and chariots of fire all around Elisha" (2 Kings 6:17). Elisha then asks that the army of the Arameans, who were sent to kill him, be struck with blindness, and he leads them away to Samaria. Jesus says, "Do you think that I cannot appeal to my Father, and he will at once send me more than twelve legions of angels?" (Matthew 26:53). These powers are real, whether we think often of them or not, and they aid those of good heart in need whether or not we understand who they are, for they are humble (the good ones, anyhow), as Jesus is humble.

Of all those who walk upon Middle-earth, the Elves are the closest in kind to the Valar, of whom Elbereth is the greatest. Certain Elves are able to dwell in two places at once, both in the Blessed Realm, toward which they sail as they flee the power of

the Dark Lord, and in the world of Hobbits. Therefore is Glorfindel able to call upon his own otherworldly power to drive the
Black Riders into the rush and roar of the Greyflood.

Others who have the power to help are only human, and not
always much to look at. Having accepted Strider as their friend, the
hobbits have to trust him through the Midgewater Marsh (much as
Sam and Frodo will follow another, less trustworthy guide through
more desperate marshes later on). Strider is not able to save Frodo
from the blade of the Ringwraiths, but he has knowledge enough of
healing to keep him alive until they reach Rivendell, where Elrond,
Master Healer, is able to bring the Ring-bearer back from the brink
of death.

So already Frodo is wounded, all but mortally, before his course
is even fully set, and there is still a long and arduous journey
ahead of him. In short, he is already defeated, but that in no way
deters him; with hope or without hope, he is willing to lay down
his life to attempt the quest set before him, and that is all that the
powers above can ask of anyone.

Sometimes the greatest challenge we face is to trust in and
accept the help we are offered. When we do not like the look of
the helper, or cannot in fact see the Helper, when we do not
know the end to which we travel and our task seems more than
impossible, we may be encouraged to remember Elisha and his
confidence in the unseen, and Frodo, whose ability to trust is
sufficient for the task.

Part Two

A Good Beginning

Book II in *The Fellowship of the Ring*

VI

Perspective

ISTORY IS A TWO-EDGED SWORD, and in some instances it is a broken sword. Like Narsil, the sword that broke under Isildur in the first war against Sauron, the races of the West are sundered, becoming more and more insular, so that few take interest in the doings of the others. Like Narsil, that diversity is reforged in Rivendell, so that what was scattered is once more united. Aragorn renames it Andúril, but it is still a two-edged sword.

The history set before the Council unites them in revealing that their separate problems are part of the same conflict, but it also divides, recalling old grievances between Elves and Dwarves and leading to an argument between Aragorn and Boromir over whose task has been more thankless and necessary. Gandalf warns them that if all such grievances are to be aired in that set-

ting, then the Council may as well be abandoned, for it is important to make a distinction between those whose mistakes are the
result of malice and those whose shortcomings are just that:
results of the imperfections that are the heirloom and weregild of
us all.

In the recounting of this history, many who had seemed familiar are shown to be strange and awesome. Gandalf the kindly
wizard, friend to Hobbits and master of fireworks, is actually
much more: a great mover of deeds. Elrond Halfelven, lord of the
Last Homely House west of the mountains, has witnessed three
ages of the world and was present when Isildur cut the Ring from
Sauron's hand. Aragorn the stern Ranger, travel-worn and weary,
is the heir of kings.

Even Gollum, the vile, famished creature who held the Ring in
secret beneath the Misty Mountains, is seen in a new light when
it is revealed that he was once part of a large family of ordinary
folk akin to Hobbits. When Gandalf almost despaired of finding
the creature and filling in his part of the history, Aragorn urged
him to continue the hunt even though it seemed too late and
other important matters were vying for attention. Had the hunt
not continued and eventually been successful, their understanding of the Ring's effect on those of small power and wisdom, like
Bilbo and Frodo, would have been greatly diminished. They
would not have known, for instance, that Hobbits don't fade as
rapidly as others and that they have enormous innate power to
resist the Ring's effects.

Knowledge of the past and the perspective it provides are
essential for making decisions in the present. But in order for

knowledge and perspective to be effective in the fight against evil, long discussions of history and ensuing debates must eventually end in action. Since history reveals that the Ring cannot be used for good but is wholly evil, the Council decides that the only right course lies in attempting its destruction. Frodo must journey to Mordor and throw the Ring into the fires of Mount Doom, where it was forged.

History can be boring, full of names that mean little to us and deeds that we don't understand. When trying to learn it, we may find ourselves joining Bilbo in calling for an early lunch. However, a sense of history gives us the foresight to see ourselves as part of a grander scheme, so that we do not take thought only for ourselves and our times but strive to make decisions that will stand forever and for all peoples. Thus the Council refuses to throw the Ring into the Sea, knowing that oceans shift, and that merely hiding the Ring will not destroy Sauron but will only prolong his weakened state until the Ring is once more recovered, even if that time is millions of years hence. It is a difficult lesson, for the problems that face us today, of dwindling resources and rampant pollution, are all too conveniently swept under the carpet of sea and land, where they can only fester without remedy until a generation arises that will take thought for all time.

The Bible is a book of disturbing, even confusing stories, unpronounceable names and the terror of God's consuming wrath. It is an ancient document whose history spans thousands of years, but we need to understand it, the Old Testament as well as the New, for the one sheds light on the other, just as the long history of the Ring sheds light on the situation the Council currently faces. History can show us what is important to keep and what is important to cast away, so that we can see the hand of him who saves and learn to trust him through all the turmoils of this age.

Even in the darkness of the mines, Gandalf takes time out to learn some history when the Fellowship comes to Balin's tomb. For all the good it does him.

VII

COMMUNITY

OMMUNITY IS A DIFFERENT entity from friendship, both stronger in its diversity and weaker (at least in the beginning) in its bonds. Its membership is often arbitrarily, even artificially chosen, either by accident of geography, history and chance, as with a church or the Council of Elrond, or by selection, as with a jury or the Nine Walkers.

Because of its diversity, the community at Rivendell is able to send out scouts to scour the land and learn of any movements of the Enemy while the companions who are to set out with the Ring can rest and make other preparations. To fulfill the tale of the Nine Walkers (chosen to match the nine Ringwraiths), Elrond seeks to include representatives from each of the major people groups present. Thus Legolas, Gimli and Boromir are chosen, for Elves, Dwarves and Men; Aragorn and Gandalf are included because their fates are bound up with the Ring; Frodo, as the Ring-bearer, must of course be chosen, as well as Sam, who in any case cannot be separated from his master. For the other two, Elrond and Gandalf are in disagreement. Elrond wishes to send Merry and Pippin home to defend the Shire against the trials that will surely assail that land. He believes that some powerful Elf-lords would be the best choice to complete the Fellowship of the Ring. Typically (though it surprises them), Gandalf defends the desire of the young hobbits to accompany Frodo. He cannot foresee to what end they will come, but he is willing to forgo Elrond's prudent counsel in favor of the desire of friends to stick together. He honors the loyalty they have already shown, and he knows that the time has passed for trusting in might to deliver the world from evil. "Many are the strange chances of the world," Gandalf reportedly said to Elrond some years earlier, "and help oft shall come from the hands of the weak when the Wise falter" (*Silmarillion*, p. 374). It isn't that Gandalf thinks the Shire isn't worth looking after, but rather that in order for any land to be kept from utter darkness for many ages to come, the quest to destroy the Ring must succeed, and in the darkness into which they all are walking, it is better to trust to the loyalty of friends than to the power of well-meaning strangers.

The best communities are made up of friends, and in the building of this type of community Gandalf is a master. Throughout his storytelling at the Council, Gandalf refers to people as his friends. From Radagast the wizard to Butterbur the publican, Gwaihir the eagle to Shadowfax the horse, Gandalf prizes friendship far above other values.

True community is based on choice. Elrond refuses to lay a charge on any Fellowship members save Frodo, even though Gimli argues that oaths may strengthen them when the road becomes dark. It is supremely difficult to hold a community together, but force is never an option. In the dread toward which Frodo travels, oaths may do no more than break the spirits of those who wish to follow him but haven't the strength.

Together the Fellowship fights off wolves, braves the storms of the Redhorn Gate and dares the Mines of Moria. All of these things are well beyond the strengths of the four hobbits who set out from the Shire, even accounting for their tremendous luck. They need the strength of Men and wizard, and the hardihood of Elf and Dwarf.

Although the artificiality of community makes it less cohesive than friendship, it can also foster unlikely friendships. Legolas and Gimli have grievances both recent and ancient, from the imprisonment of the Dwarves (one of whom was Gimli's father) in their adventure with Bilbo, to the nameless fear the Dwarves encountered in Moria, before even Legolas (perhaps) was born. Yet within the confines of the Fellowship they learn to respect and care for each other, and their friendship grows.

In this also it is Gandalf who encourages them. In a debate over which race was responsible for the waning of friendship between the two peoples, he says, "I have heard both, and I will not give judgement now. But I beg you two, Legolas and Gimli, at least to be friends, and to help me. I need you both" (I:362-63).

The Shire, Rivendell and later Lothlórien are havens of community, oases of light in a land of growing darkness. Community keeps history alive, provides succor to strangers and fosters friendships amid its people. They may survive for thousands of years doing nothing more, and still they will be beacons of light, with the ability to bless the whole world.

VIII

SACRIFICE

N ITS HIGHEST FORM, sacrifice is an extraordinary virtue, and those who attain it are called martyrs. But there is a more ordinary expression of this virtue that is nonetheless extremely powerful and often invisible. This is the sacrifice Jesus asks of all who would follow him—that they leave everything they own. The hobbits leave behind everything that is dear and familiar, all that they have known of the world. Boromir, Legolas and Gimli leave behind homelands that are under threat of war. Aragorn has been postponing for years a love affair with Arwen, whom he leaves behind at Rivendell.

Anything worthwhile requires this kind of sacrifice. Whether it's leaving home to go on a mission trip, taking time out of a busy schedule to do volunteer work or staying at home to raise children, relinquishing things that are important for the sake of things that seem more important is the only way for the world to become a better place.

Distinguishing between "important" and "more important" is, of course, no easy task, but it comes down to a matter of calling. Boromir left the wars on his own border in response to a dream. His brother had the same dream several times, but Boromir took the journey to Imladris upon himself. The task of judging whether this was his true calling or not resides in his own heart and falls only secondarily to the outside observer. The question "what if" is impossible to answer.

Gandalf's entire purpose in life is to stand against Sauron and encourage others to join him, and so it might seem that he has little to sacrifice in joining the Company. In truth, his entire life is a gift to the peoples of the West. He has never had a permanent residence, his only apparent possession is his staff, and many of his closest friends are members of the Fellowship. Like Paul the apostle, he endeavors to be all things to all people, to suffer imprisonment and hard journeys and to light a fire in the hearts of others.

Although he is the acknowledged leader of the expedition, Gandalf never hesitates to sacrifice his authority. When they come to the choice between Moria and the Redhorn Pass, he does not insist that Aragorn and the others bow to his wisdom but agrees to attempt Caradhras. He warns against the use of fire, but when the choice is between fire and death, he not only allows a fire to be built but uses the power within him to start it for them, even though doing so betrays his presence to anyone in the area who can read the signs.

When the Balrog comes, wisdom might counsel that Gandalf save Frodo and himself, for they are the most obviously important members of the Fellowship, and the Ring-bearer will need Gandalf's help on the long road ahead. The rest are expendable. But he is not their leader so much as their friend, and like Jesus, he has the love that will lay down his life for his friends. He stands before the Balrog, Durin's Bane, breaks the demon's sword and shatters the bridge beneath him.

He does not stand like Boromir fighting Orcs at the bridge of Osgiliath, spurred on by thoughts of glory and honor. He stands like an old man, weary and alone, who knows he has met his match. When the thongs of the Balrog's whips lash around his ankles and he grabs in vain at the shards of the bridge, his final words are neither screams of despair nor cries for help, but words of concern for his friends. "'Fly, you fools!' he cried, and was gone" (I:393).

Wise generals lead from the rear, so that in the clash of arms their leadership may not be lost. They alone have the strategy of the whole war, and their army cannot afford to lose them in the heat of a single battle. But none of us are called to sacrifice others to safeguard ourselves, no matter how important we may seem. The proper position of leadership is in front, partaking fully in the dangers of the lowliest of soldiers. This is what Jesus did, and it is the height of foolishness. May we, in our weakness, be granted access to such heights.

IX

WONDER

HEN THE FIRST WAVE of weeping passes for Gandalf, Gimli insists that Frodo (and the inseparable Sam) join him in gazing upon the waters of Kheled-zâram. This is not callousness on the dwarf's part—he has just learned that all the Dwarves that set out to reclaim Moria are dead. Thus the Mines are a monument of loss to him, but his appreciation of beauty is undiminished. It is one of the marks of his people that they will dig through rock to uncover the precious things of the earth. The sense of wonder that draws him to the Mirrormere is the same that encouraged Gandalf as they prepared to enter Moria, and is entirely appropriate.

The chief wonder of the Mirrormere is that it reflects only mountains and stars. "Of their own stooping forms, no shadow could be seen" (I:395). There are some things that mark not the

fleeting bustle of our time, neither the triumphs nor the trage-
dies. They will survive whatever chances befall the times, and
will not be moved until the earth itself is removed.

"For now we see in a mirror, dimly" (1 Corinthians 13:12).
When someone we love dies unexpectedly, or something we had
assumed was immovable is shattered, it can shake the very founda-
tions of our souls. The eternal in this context may be cold comfort,
but it reminds us that although we ourselves may fail, there is a
beauty and a significance that will survive. This is the hope and
doom of Lothlórien—that the glory of the place must inevitably
fade, yet that there is a higher glory its inhabitants can turn to
when their home finally falls. It is a bittersweet consolation at best,
but it is enough, and the Elves are wise enough that they will sacrifice their home for the redemption of Middle-earth.

When the Fellowship reaches Lothlórien they are blindfolded
and led for a day and a half without sight. Frodo finds that his
other senses are sharpened, so that when at last his eyes are
uncovered, he nearly drowns in beauty and can do nothing but
stand and stare, until Sam says, "I feel as if I was *inside* a song, if
you take my meaning" (I:415). When Frodo places his hand on a
tree, "he felt a delight in wood and the touch of it, neither as a for-
ester nor as a carpenter; it was the delight of the living tree itself"
(I:415).

Lothlórien is a sort of earthly paradise, an undecaying garden
set in the midst of a falling world. Like the Garden of Eden, it is
full of magic and wonder, but also of danger. The companions are

cleansed by wading through the Nimrodel, but the choices they
face in Lothlórien's unspoiled wood have all the more power to
stain.

Galadriel's mirror is Kheled-zâram's opposite, for while the
Mirrormere reflects only that which is sure, Galadriel's bit of
"Elf-magic" shows any number of things that are not and some
that will never be. But she says, "Seeing is both good and perilous" (I:429). Frodo and Sam see many things in the mirror, and
while it may not be obvious what good it offers them, the peril
before them is clarified.

There is wonder too in the sacrifice of Gandalf, in the indis-
putable fact that one so wise and powerful cared more for each
one of his friends than for anything else that belonged to him.
This, amid their memories of all he did and was to them,
increases their appreciation of the beauty of Lothlórien, that it
gives them the chance to honor his memory.

The Lord of the Rings is a tale of desperate struggles against
insurmountable odds, but it is suffused throughout with a deep
sense of wonder. The landscape the companions journey through,
the people they encounter and the friendships they develop keep
alive in them a sense that the world is good and beautiful and well
worth saving. Even when Gandalf is lost to them, they can begin to
find healing and rest from their grief in the wonders of Middle-
earth.

X

TEMPTATION

HEN THE COMPANIONS first meet the Lord and Lady of Lothlórien, Galadriel says, "Your Quest stands upon the edge of a knife. Stray but a little and it will fail, to the ruin of all. Yet hope remains while all the Company is true" (I:422). She then proceeds to look into each one of their hearts, with a perceptiveness that shames them. If Lothlórien is as full of unstained beauty as the Garden of Eden, then Galadriel is either the serpent or the sword-wielding seraph.

Temptation in itself is not altogether bad. In testing we learn the quality of each other's character. Only Legolas and Aragorn are able to hold the Lady's gaze for long, for they are the most confident in their motives. Sam is the one who blushes quickest; when he is questioned about it, he adds to the Edenic imagery by saying, "I felt as if I hadn't got nothing on, and I didn't like it"

(I:422). Nevertheless he is the only one willing to reveal the choice he felt he had been given. Boromir, on the other hand, reveals his pride and lack of understanding by questioning Galadriel's own motives in testing them thus, and though he will not reveal what his own temptation was, he badgers Frodo to say what the Lady seemed to offer him.

It is good to know what temptations our friends most struggle with, and even better to share our own. The knowledge, so long as it is neither forced nor judged, can draw a community closer together, increasing our trust in each other and giving us strength. Conversely, it can show us where our friends are likely to falter and perhaps prepare us somewhat for the consequences should they do so. And there is joy and freedom in finding ourselves and our friends strong in resisting that which tempts us most.

It is difficult for us to understand how temptation can be good, since from the beginning we have succumbed to it. Yet it was not present in the Garden of Eden for our downfall but for our building up. It is the same in Lothlórien and with Galadriel. As Aragorn says, "There is in her and in this land no evil, unless a Man bring it hither himself. Then let him beware!" (I:423). Here indeed Boromir's brother, Faramir, would almost certainly have fared better, but then all manner of things would have been different, and who can say what then the ultimate outcome would have been, either for the better or for the worse?

Later on Galadriel brings Frodo and Sam to gaze, if they will, into her mirror, though she knows that it is likely to frighten them and to tempt them further to turn from their path. It is almost too much for poor Sam. To see the Shire's trees cut down, homes dug up and his elderly father sent packing cuts him in two, so that he wants to continue with Frodo and return home at the same time. But he is not really in any danger from temptation, for his heart is open and pliable, and he knows his duty to his master. He knows he has "something to do before the end" (I:118), and he will not turn aside from it, no matter that his heart may break.

Frodo, on the other hand, is the one chosen, and for him there can be no turning back. He sees many things in the mirror, but finally there is only the Eye, searching for him, implacable, pitiless and hungry. Faced with this horrific image of the evil toward which he is traveling, he offers the Ring to Galadriel, just as he had offered it to Gandalf when he first learned the nature of his burden.

Galadriel laughs. She is akin to Gandalf, after all—an angel and not a serpent. If she is more tempted by the Ring than he was, she is also able to forswear it with a lighter heart. She is not a temptress but one who understands the nature of temptation. She has a long history, and it has not all been strictly honorable, but she has gained wisdom from her mistakes, and she knows that laughter is the surest defense against temptation. Her only wish is "that what should be shall be" (I:431), and she will not grasp at the power to change it. She will diminish, and her land with her, and she will be content.

Galadriel gives each of the companions a gift before they leave Lothlórien, but it may be that her greatest and most perilous gift was given upon their first meeting. Temptation, successfully overcome, strengthens the will, but succumbing to temptation, even in thought, leads to evil.

XI

FAILURE

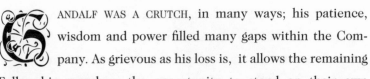ANDALF WAS A CRUTCH, in many ways; his patience, wisdom and power filled many gaps within the Company. As grievous as his loss is, it allows the remaining Fellowship members the opportunity to stand on their own shaky feet. Which is also to say that it gives them the opportunity to fall down. The important thing to remember about falling down, though, is simply that it offers the chance of standing up again.

As they flee from Moria, Aragorn in his haste leaves Sam and Frodo lagging behind; he forgets that they are both wounded. Gandalf would never have been so absent-minded, and upon discovering his error Aragorn no doubt is aware of this. He feels utterly inadequate to take Gandalf's place, and yet he needs to learn how to lead. He had hoped that he would be free to accompany Boromir to Minas Tirith, but now it appears that he will have to lead Frodo to Mordor. Gandalf may have felt himself expendable enough to sacrifice his life for the Company, but Aragorn does not feel that Gandalf was expendable, and so, in taking up his mantle, he does not believe that he himself is. This cuts him in two, like Sam looking into Galadriel's mirror, but his heart is not as sure as Sam's, or rather he rebels against it, for his heart tells him to continue to Minas Tirith, but his mind tells him it would be cruel and cowardly to send Frodo on to Mordor without him. This is true enough, but between duty and calling it is never easy to decide. Aragorn's indecision is the beginning of the Company's failure.

The temptation of Galadriel has awakened in Boromir the pride of his father and of his people, and he gives in to the temptation (that in truth was there all along). He tries to force his will upon Frodo, betrays his trust and gives way to madness. His hope is in the strength of Gondor and not in the folly which the Council of Elrond has called wisdom. He tries to convince Frodo of this perspective, and when words fail, he tries to wrest the Ring from the tiny hobbit, which drives Frodo to put on the Ring and disappear.

By virtue of contrast, we see at last the true measure of the strength of Gandalf and Galadriel, for here is the power of the Ring revealed in full. Simply being near the Ring for so long, Boromir has become convinced that it should belong to him. This is the temptation that Gandalf resisted for eighty years. He refused its call even when the Ring was freely offered. Boromir has no such strength, for all his talk of the steadfastness of Men.

Frodo flees to Amon Hen, the Hill of Sight, where he sees many things, but he finds his gaze drawn inexorably East, to Barad-dûr, whence he can feel the eye of the Dark Lord become suddenly aware of him and begin hungrily seeking his position. Like an echo of the wisest voice among them come the words "Take it off! Take it off! Fool, take it off! Take off the Ring!" (I:472).

Caught between the Voice and the Eye, Frodo writhes, tortured, but then returns to himself, a simple hobbit; he sensibly takes off the Ring, and so the ultimate failure is diverted, for a while. Perceiving that the power of the Ring is at work in the Company, he resolves to remove the danger from them and set his face toward Mordor alone.

Boromir returns at length to the Company, little understanding the danger he has placed them in. When he tells them that Frodo put on the Ring and ran away, the others immediately fall into a madness of panic and race in every direction, calling Frodo's name. Aragorn, powerless to stop them, sends Boromir to look after Merry and Pippin and takes off after Sam himself.

Boromir is able to take orders, even though, as the son of the Steward, he is more used to giving commands. Aragorn, though of higher rank and lineage, is not so level-headed in this instance. He overtakes Sam quickly but just as quickly leaves him behind, just as he had when leading the Company away from Moria. His desire is to sit on Amon Hen, urged on not only by the hope that Frodo will be found there but by a pride that makes him swell as he sees the statues of his ancestors guarding the river.

Alone, Sam comes to his senses. He puzzles out his master's

mind and runs headlong back to the boats. Seeing that one is pulling away seemingly empty from the bank, he leaps into the river, heedless of the rushing water he has feared since childhood. Frodo rescues him and tries to convince him to stay behind but fails. It is the final failure in the *Fellowship of the Ring*, but this one makes Frodo laugh. They set out apparently untroubled by the fact that the fate of the entire world is now resting on the wisdom, might and resolve of two hobbits.

Failure is the end of almost every good beginning. God himself had to contend with it almost immediately after creation. But that did not stop him from continuing on, determined to finish what he started. Perhaps the greatest temptation of all is to surrender when our plans fail, but in retrospect it is almost always possible to see how initial disappointments and failures led in the end to a greater success than we had initially believed possible.

> The stone that the builders rejected
>   has become the chief cornerstone.
> This is the LORD's doing;
>   it is marvelous in our eyes. (Psalm 118:22-23)

Part Three

A New Beginning

Book III in *The Two Towers*

XII

ATONEMENT

AILURE IS NOT TO BE WONDERED AT. What is marvelous is when those who have fallen nevertheless pick themselves up and continue on. When we refuse to surrender to defeat, our failures may be redeemed and our character rebuilt. It is rarely possible to make it as if our failures had never happened or to erase their consequences, but it is almost always possible to atone for our mistakes and move on in the hope that "all things work together for good for those who love God, who are called according to his purpose" (Romans 8:28).

Boromir not only fails but betrays. Full of pride and trusting in his own strength, he is overpowered by the Ring, and he believes the lie that it should belong to him and that he can do great things with it. This is the crucial breaking point of the Fellowship, and it is almost the end of the entire quest. Boromir's sin is grievous, as he realizes as soon as the fit passes, yet he wanders for close to an hour, too ashamed to return to the Company, assuming perhaps that Frodo has run to them for protection and so they already know all that he has done.

For all his shortcomings, however—his rashness, his disdain for wise counsel and his pride—he is a brave and honest Man. He does not run away to return alone to Minas Tirith, where he could make up a story to explain his departure from the Fellowship that would almost certainly be believed over the word of a Halfling. Instead he returns to face the Company. His pride is purged, and though he does not tell the Company everything, he gives them enough information to send them into a panic, running off heedless of Aragorn's shouts. Boromir is a soldier, and he alone awaits Aragorn's orders and obeys. He catches up with Merry and Pippin and defends them with his life.

When Aragorn finds him, he is sitting against a tree, pierced by many arrows. His sword, though broken, is still in his hand. He says, "I tried to take the Ring from Frodo. I am sorry. I have paid" (II:18). He says that Merry and Pippin were still alive when last he saw them. Then he says goodbye: "Farewell, Aragorn. Go to Minas Tirith and save my people. I have failed." Aragorn, perhaps understanding the nature of his real battle, tells him he has achieved a rare kind of victory. Boromir smiles, then dies.

Confession is an essential step in atoning for our sins, and from God's point of view it is enough. "Then I acknowledged my sin to you, / and I did not hide my iniquity; / I said, 'I will confess my transgressions to the LORD,' / and you forgave the guilt of my sin" (Psalm 32:5). But oftentimes we desire something more, some way to prove ourselves worthy again. And sometimes God grants us the opportunity to do so.

Atonement does not always directly help the one we have sinned against. It does not always help anyone at all. Had Boromir run off with Aragorn, he could have been of greater help in tracking the Orcs after Merry and Pippin were captured than he was in giving his life to defend them. To the living we may say that atonement is not necessary, that only repentance and humility are required. But to the dead who have given their lives to pay for their sins, the question whether they were right to do so is irrelevant. Boromir died well, in the defense of those whose safety was his charge, and he is thereby worthy of honor.

One gift he does impart to Merry and Pippin is the gift of significance. It is the same gift that Gandalf has given to all of them, but Boromir's is all the more powerful in being specific to the two young hobbits. Boromir has acted as if their lives were of greater importance than his own. Their significance has been there all along, but it has been unbearably heightened by a mighty warrior's sacrifice, and now they have the task of living up to it, of proving Boromir right.

Aragorn has also failed. His pride is not so great as Boromir's, and his wisdom is greater, but he has a weakness common to humanity. Both he and Boromir have been fond of reminding people that but for the strength and watchfulness of themselves and their people, the simpler people of the world would long since have fallen prey to unimaginable horrors. Yet here in the wild, with only four such simple people in their care—two apiece—they fail. Boromir atones for his betrayal with his death. Aragorn must take the longer road and atone with his life.

If the breaking of the Fellowship accomplishes one good thing, it is that Aragorn's heart "speaks clearly at last" (II:25). Though the Orcs have a tremendous head start, after Boromir's funeral he decides he will chase them. Legolas and Gimli join him, and together they set out, a Man, an Elf and a Dwarf, with the purpose of overtaking a company of Orcs and either rescuing Merry and Pippin or perishing in the attempt.

Tirelessly they run, set free from the weight of uncertainty, their path clear and easy to follow. With each league that passes, a little more guilt and shame falls by the way. Within four days, after forty-five leagues, their souls are virtually clean. They meet the Rohirrim and are given horses, and in the eaves of Fangorn they are at last absolved by one they thought they had lost.

Atonement is hard work; this is obvious to the most casual observer. What is less widely recognized is that atonement is also a great joy. It is the working out of the creative process by which our shortcomings are overcome and our failures redeemed. After Peter denies Jesus three times, the risen Lord gives him a chance to affirm three times his love. Each time Jesus charges him to care for his people, to feed his sheep. Thus Peter's shame is lifted.

The chase of the Three Hunters is of no use to Merry and Pippin except that they pick up Pippin's brooch with the hope of returning it to him. But it strengthens the Hunters, hardens them and purifies them, and brings them to Edoras in time to ride to war.

XIII

SUFFERING

ERRY AND PIPPIN HAVE little to atone for. What shortcomings they have have been more than made up for by their mere presence in the desperate Company; they know what the dangers are and yet still want to follow Frodo into whatever further dangers may arise. But they also need to be strengthened, hardened and brought to the place they are most needed. They have to be shown how strong and resourceful and tough they can be. Is there any other way to accomplish these things except through suffering? "Many are the afflictions of the righteous, / but the LORD rescues them from them all" (Psalm 34:19). It is through suffering that we learn who we really are.

When Pippin regains consciousness among the Orcs, he feels neither strong nor resourceful and wonders what use he had hoped to be in joining Frodo. He feels that he has been "just a nuisance: a passenger, a piece of luggage" (II:56). That will not change magically, but he does what he can. When a fight breaks out among the Orcs and one of them falls on top of him, slain, he uses the edge of the knife held fast by the dead hand to cut the cords binding his wrists, and he has the wits to loop them around again, so that they seem to be intact. It is not the most cunning of tricks, but it is a start.

Pippin begins from Merry to learn what Hobbits are capable of. "Good old Merry," he thinks (II:55) while trying to piece together his memories of the attack, recalling that Merry cut the hands off several Orcs. When they are each given a jolt of orc-liquor, Merry stands, "looking pale but grim and defiant" (II:60). This is not how Hobbits are commonly described.

Now that Pippin has the use of his feet, and after the success of his first attempt to rely on his own wits, he decides to take another, bolder chance. The vision of Strider running behind them moves him to leave behind something that will tell the Ranger he is not running in vain. Having lost everything, all his baggage as well as his freedom, he does not stint to drop the one precious thing left to him: the brooch that Galadriel gave him. The gesture seems futile, as he supposes rationally that the others of the Company have continued with Frodo. He pays for his courage with the lash of a whip, but it is another step toward understanding the power that lies within him. As Aragorn tells him later, "One who cannot cast away a treasure at need is in fetters" (II:199).

Anyone can suffer, but it takes a stout heart to suffer well. Pippin never loses his simple Hobbit sense, nor does he succumb to the temptation to use his suffering as an excuse to sully himself. When the Orcs throw food at them, he eats the "stale grey bread hungrily, but not the meat. He was famished, but not yet so famished as to eat flesh flung to him by an Orc" (II:63). The fact that he is suffering cruelly at the hands of Orcs does not give him license to act like an Orc, and so, like Job, he maintains his purity in the midst of his suffering.

When at last the Riders of Rohan have caught up with them and Grishnákh the Orc is pawing at them, Pippin takes one last gamble. Using a subtlety of wit far beyond what Grishnákh believes him capable of, he insinuates that he has the Ring and will help the Orc find it if he will loose their bonds. The ruse does not have the intended effect, any more than the chase of the Three Hunters accomplishes what Aragorn purposed, but it is enough to convince Grishnákh to attempt to carry them off. When he is slain, the hobbits, thanks to Pippin's untied hands, are able to escape the massacre of the Orcs and crawl into the woods.

Merry and Pippin were simply friends of Frodo, along for moral support but possessed of no special skills or abilities. Now at last, hundreds of miles from the Shire, they find they have the strength to survive capture by Orcs and escape without assistance from their friends. Not that they do it alone—the Rohirrim take care of the Orcs, and there is that mysterious other presence giving Pippin his vision of Strider and guiding the arrow that pierced Grishnákh's hand. But they would have been nothing but a pile of charred bones mingled with those of the Orcs had they not discovered that they too can be strong when the need arises.

"Suffering produces endurance, and endurance produces character, and character produces hope, and hope does not disappoint us" (Romans 5:3-5).

XIV

RESURRECTION

F COURSE. OF COURSE it is Gandalf, not Saruman, whom the Three Hunters meet in Fangorn. Of course Gandalf is not lost forever before the first book is even over. According to the timeline in appendix B, he battled the Balrog for ten days, and he did indeed die. It was almost three weeks before he returned to life on top of Mount Celebdil, and three more days before Gwaihir the Eagle found him and bore him to Lothlórien. He refuses to speak of the roads his spirit traveled in those dark days, but he does say, "Naked I was sent back—for a brief time, until my task was done" (II:125).

Gandalf's virtues are extraordinary, but his love for ordinary virtues is boundless, and one of his greatest strengths is his ability to inspire and encourage such workaday virtues in others. His death and resurrection have increased his joy and mirth as well as his confidence and power. He absolves Aragorn of his mistakes in leading the Company, saying, "You chose amid doubts the path that seemed right: the choice was just, and it has been rewarded. For so we have met in time, who otherwise might have met too late" (II:123).

Resurrection, like sacrifice, is an experience few of us are called to in the highest sense, but we may have a taste of it whenever we wake up from our dull dreaming days to the realization that we are in the midst of a glorious struggle and that we have been given more power than we knew.

King Théoden, like so many of us, has lived long under the influence of lies—lies that he is weak, old, that there is nothing he can do but guard what strength he has left. Gandalf arrives with the intention of imparting some of his new life into the old king. He stops the mouth of Gríma Wormtongue and invites Théoden for a walk. He shows him the storm Gríma has taught him to fear, but the ray of light also, and whispers to him of their secret hope. He counsels him to cast aside his prop and grasp a sword instead, and to trust the trustworthy more than the craven.

These simple actions transform Théoden from a dotard into a warrior king. The essence of the ordinary form of resurrection is this: "To cast aside regret and fear. To do the deed at hand" (II:144).

It is nearly impossible to wake ourselves up. However hard we strain at our bootstraps, we will rarely lift ourselves up off the ground. We need help, someone to shake us, someone who recognizes the lulling whisperers for who they are—servants of the enemy—and can shut their mouths. Someone who will show us the situation as it really stands. In both cases the information is coming from an outside source, but here is one way to distinguish between the trustworthy voice and the liars. The truth is that the situation is desperate but there is hope; the lie is either that there is no situation at all or that there is no hope. The liar tells us there is nothing we can do. The trustworthy tell us that what little we have to give is desperately needed.

Merry and Pippin have experienced a minor resurrection themselves, though not their first. They have awakened from their three days in the belly of a company of Orcs (much as they were awakened by Tom Bombadil from Old Man Willow and the Barrow Wight) and discovered that their hope was not in vain. With wonderful symmetry, they meet a relative of Old Man Willow, Treebeard the Ent, but whereas Old Man Willow lulled them both to sleep, Merry and Pippin manage to wake old Treebeard up.

Ents are not a hasty folk. They are like Shirefolk in that way. But they are an awesome force when roused. Treebeard has long pondered the evils he has seen, trees cut down and left to rot, Orcs roaming freely through his woods. He has slowly been growing angry, but up until the hobbits arrive he has taken no action. Merry and Pippin rouse him with a very simple method: storytelling. They tell him their own story, and Treebeard comes to understand that "there is something very big going on" (II:88).

What little they are able to tell him of Saruman fills in the gaps in his knowledge, and he understands that Saruman is wishing to set himself up as a major power in whatever the very big thing is. Simply talking it out, giving voice to his long slow thoughts, builds up his anger at last to the bursting point. "Curse him, root and branch!" he shouts, pounding on the table so that jets of flame erupt from the bowls of water. "I have been idle. I have let things slip. It must stop!" (II:90). Wrath, one of the most neglected of virtues (in Western cultures at least), is often the missing key to the door of our tombs.

Treebeard, in turn, wakes up the other Ents and whole groves of trees. Thus as a direct result of Merry and Pippin's suffering at the hands of the Orcs, the young hobbits have aroused the only force in that corner of Middle-earth with the power to defeat the Orcs and mount an assault on Isengard.

Every morning (or whenever it is we get up) is a resurrection of sorts, but many of us (I'd say "most," but that seems presumptuous) rarely come fully awake. Recovering alcoholics speak of a "moment of clarity," when the long bad dream brought on by their drinking is finally revealed for what it really is. Anyone in the grip of some longstanding sin may experience something similar. In the grace of such a moment, we are given what may be a final chance to rouse ourselves and take the actions we've suspected for some time need to be taken.

It is easy to move through our lives half-asleep, always waiting for a more convenient time, never accomplishing what we had hoped. For a while that is acceptable, though hardly what even we would wish for ourselves, but when the time comes we will know it, and then we will have to choose whether it is worth waking up, taking hold of the power we find within in us and harnessing the power in our communities, putting a stop to the evil we have too long been content merely to watch with disapproval.

But let's think through our actions before we attempt them. There's no need to be hasty.

XV

HUMILITY

UMILITY, AT LEAST IN PART, is the act of giving and receiving true names. Not the names that pride would have us accept that are not ours by right, but neither the names that shame would have us accept, which may contain a grain of truth but are not the whole truth.

Gríma, Saruman's disciple, reminds Théoden of his advanced years, of how tired he is and how little can be done. In so doing he is feeding him names, which Théoden then takes on himself and comes to believe are essentially true. Gandalf's method of healing him is simply to return to Théoden his true name: king.

Gandalf exposes Gríma's lies and commands him to grovel on his belly. This is not pride or bullying on Gandalf's part, for he counsels that Gríma should be given a horse and that the direction he rides should be noted. "By his choice you shall judge him" (I:147). Humility is not the same as meekness, and Gandalf in his power and wisdom is able to render true names. Théoden he names king; Gríma he names snake.

When he presents the palantír to Aragorn, Gandalf surprises everyone by kneeling down and saying, "Receive it, lord! in earnest of other things that shall be given back" (II:236). Even though Gandalf knows his own true name, even though he is a being far greater than any of those he walks among, he does not lord his power over others but bows before the king.

Gandalf and Saruman are called Wizards, but this is not their true name. Their powers are great and mysterious, and in most respects equal, but the greater part of Gandalf's power lies in his ability to speak truth, whereas Saruman's power is in twisting the truth and being able to persuade others of lies. When those of evil intention are humbled, their spells are broken. This is dramatically illustrated in the confrontation with Saruman, when Gandalf names himself Gandalf the White and calls Saruman Fool, who had been chief of the Council of the Wise, and strips him of all color.

One of the effects of Saruman's wizardry is to make all other voices sound rough and unpleasant. Gimli, as the first to respond to Saruman's kind-sounding enchantment, is aided by the natural harshness of his own voice. The truth he speaks thereby does not sound so strange. Théoden, in his newfound humility, is able to answer Saruman, "A lesser son of greater sires I am. But I do not need to lick your fingers" (II:219). Théoden has accepted his true name, and Saruman's lies have no more power over him.

As Galadriel has already shown, laughter is one of the chief tools of humility. As Saruman tries to force Gandalf to accept the name Pride, it seems to all who listen that it is only natural that the two of them should ascend to the tower and speak of matters too high for ordinary folk. So great is the power of Saruman's last effort that even Théoden is sure Gandalf will betray them. "Then Gandalf laughed. The fantasy vanished like a puff of smoke" (II:220).

Humility is an elusive virtue, as C. S. Lewis describes in *The Screwtape Letters*. Indeed I am all too familiar with the twists and turns of it, and in writing this chapter I have come to question the very nature of this book. As the devil Screwtape says, "All virtues are less formidable to [demons] once the man is aware that he has them, but this is specially true of humility." Would Tolkien appreciate my taking his book apart as I have, laying bare the virtues within it? Do I consider myself to be an expert in virtues, that I would dare to write such a book? When such questions begin to circle in my mind, I try to remember Gandalf's laughter, and Screwtape's warning to his nephew Wormwood not to push such questions too far "for fear you awake [the person's] sense of humour and proportion, in which case he will merely laugh at you and go to bed" (p. 301).

XVI

PROVIDENCE

ANDALF, LOOKING TOWARD THE EAST, says a curious thing: "I am Gandalf, Gandalf the White, but Black is mightier still" (II:123). The statement recalls the opening verses of John: "The light shines in the darkness, and the darkness did not overcome it" (John 1:5). What is curious is that it seems reasonable to expect the light to do more than withstand an assault of darkness, to expect it to overcome. If God is omnipotent, the Creator of the universe, then surely the light that represents him is greater than the darkness that opposes him. On this Middle-earth, darkness takes flight at the coming of the dawn, but out in space, in the vast expanses we refer to as the universe, all is black, and the stars, for all their glory, each as great or greater than our sun, look small and dim in comparison.

God has chosen weakness to represent him. In his arsenal of weaknesses one of his chief weapons is Providence.

At its most elemental, Providence is evident in the natural order of Middle-earth. As the ultimate expression of the power of light, the Sun plays a significant part in the adventure. As the Hunters run, Legolas says, "Yet do not cast all hope away. Tomorrow is unknown. Rede oft is found at the rising of the sun" (II:37). Indeed the following morning they meet Éomer and his Men. In the battle of Helm's Deep, Aragorn takes up Legolas's words and says, "Yet dawn is ever the hope of Men" (II:167). When dawn approaches, he stands upon the battlement to greet it and to face the Orcs, who jeer at his hope. Yet dawn arrives, Théoden and Aragorn set out from Hornburg to make a last, desperate stand, and at that moment "light sprang into the sky. Night departed" (II:171). And the light of the Sun reveals the forest of Huorns that have come to overwhelm and consume the Orcs.

Throughout the tale, the weather seems an active, almost proactive agent in the adventure, sometimes for evil and sometimes for good. In literary study this is called "pathetic fallacy"; here it is evidence that all the world is participating in the struggle.

Providence also works through the choices and chances of our own decisions. Though Merry and Pippin at first seemed little more than baggage, they are eventually revealed to be tremendous instruments of Providence. In providing a means for Boromir's atonement they justify Gandalf's trust in them, and for this reason alone Gandalf is glad they set out from Rivendell. They arrive in Fangorn just in time to rouse the Ents, without

whom Rohan might have fallen at the battle of Helm's Deep and Saruman would not have been defeated without much greater cost. Pippin, though he errs by looking into the Palantír, thereby saves Gandalf from making the same mistake. Even our failures can be powerful instruments of Providence.

Yet Gandalf says that "good fortune, as it is called," cannot be relied on. "You cannot count on it a second time" (II:235). As he presents the Palantír to Aragorn, he cautions him against using it precipitously. Aragorn protests that he has never acted precipitously, but Gandalf says, "Do not then stumble at the end of the road" (II:236). Providence, as the weakness of God, is a powerful force, but as Paul says to the church at Philippi: "Work out your own salvation with fear and trembling; for it is God who is at work in you, enabling you both to will and to work for his good pleasure" (Philippians 2:12-13). It is God's good work, but he has called us to participate in it fully, to hope in Providence but not to rely on it to the exclusion of our own participation.

The many battles of the Old Testament are won or lost in a variety of ways, but God is always in control of the outcome. The common thread is that those who put their trust in him will succeed, whether with many or with few, whether through clever strategies or by singing praise songs. Or by simply marching, shouting and winding trumpets, as in Jericho (Joshua 6) and Helm's Deep. The battle belongs to the Lord.

It might be pointed out that Providence is not strictly speaking a virtue. I include it because I believe it to be one of God's virtues, if you will. It is a facet of his tireless devotion to this world he has created and refuses to surrender to evil. It is a facet

also of his humility, of his wisdom, of his hope and of his mirth.
A strange dance goes on around us every day. Evil twists good
things to evil purposes, and good twists evil into greater good.
The light is indeed greater, but whereas evil seeks ever for domination and destruction, sometimes even of itself, good seeks ever
for redemption, even for those things that seem irredeemably
evil.

Part Four

Book IV in *The Two Towers*

XVII

TRUST

RODO AND THE COMPANY are charged with keeping a mighty secret. Yet they are in the service of the Truth, and so at times, according to their wisdom, certain secrets are revealed. Galadriel reveals to Frodo that she is the keeper of Nenya, one of the three Elven Rings, of which it is not permitted that any should speak. Galadriel does not feel it should be hidden from the Ring-bearer. Of all the gifts she gives, this is the most precious, for when we are trusted we become more trustworthy. Being trusted with another's secret makes us feel honored and befriended. It builds up our soul, showing us that we are not alone in the burdens we have to carry but that others stand beside us, waging the same battle, striving toward the same end.

Immediately upon leaving the Fellowship, Sam and Frodo

reach an impasse. They spend days searching for a way down from the rocky hills they've been traversing and almost give up hope of finding one. But Frodo says, "It's my doom, I think, to go to that Shadow yonder, so that a way will be found. But will good or evil show it to me?" (II:248). Alone, the two hobbits have no more hope of finding Mount Doom than Dante had of finding the deepest pit of hell. They need a guide, and since Frodo has left behind every friend save Sam, he must settle for getting help from an enemy.

So it is that when Frodo decides to take someone outside the Company into his confidence, he chooses, of all people, Gollum. Sam is amazed to hear his master confirm that they are going to Mordor. Gollum is a known friend of Orcs, and if word should get back to the enemy about their intentions, all will shortly be lost. Frodo knows all this, yet he chooses not to hide the truth.

Sméagol responds by clapping his hands to his ears and hissing, "as if such frankness, and the open speaking of the names, hurt him" (II:262). All good things hurt Gollum: the light of Sun and Moon, anything made by Elves, even simple truth. The unexpected honesty prompts him, against his will, to respond in kind, answering truthfully when Frodo asks him if he has been to Mordor, though he immediately tries to deny it.

Jesus said to the multitude, "Love your enemies, do good to those who hate you, bless those who curse you, pray for those who abuse you" (Luke 6:27-28). Before he met Gollum, Frodo did not understand this line of thinking, but in the time since he left the Shire he has witnessed firsthand the effect the Ring has, even upon people like Boromir who have never touched it. He has begun to feel the weight of it, to see how difficult it is for himself to withstand temptation, and he has felt also the horror of the searching Eye of Mordor. In short, he has begun to understand the forces that corrupted Gollum and thus has gained the ability to feel pity for him.

Frodo's trust has an immediate effect on Gollum. His voice changes, and the two hobbits see the first indication of the Sméagol still dwelling deep within the mind of Gollum. Sméagol was once something very like a hobbit, but he has been ruined by the power of the Ring and by the centuries he spent beneath the mountain. The Ring has gnawed away at his body and soul, twisting him into a mockery of a hobbit, in the same way that certain of the Elves were twisted by Sauron's master, Melkor, into the race known as Orcs (*Silmarillion*, p. 50). Gollum is loathsome, in league with Orcs, and there is even a hint that he has eaten babies (I:84). Sauron himself has tortured him and has charged him to find the Ring and return it to Barad-dûr. To say he is an untrustworthy guide is the grossest kind of understatement. He is the embodiment of the very worst that a hobbit can become.

Yet Gandalf does not think him wholly ruined. Long ago, in Frodo's sitting room, he suggested, regarding the riddle game between Gollum and Bilbo, "It was actually pleasant, I think, to hear a kindly voice again, bringing up memories of wind, and trees, and sun on the grass, and such forgotten things" (I:80).

Frodo continues to put his faith in the Providence that has seen him through all the dangers thus far, and he does not concern himself with guarding Gollum ceaselessly as Sam tries to do. He follows Gollum through the Dead Marshes and right up to the gates of Mordor, then again to the Tower of Cirith Ungol and the horrible tunnel. As Gandalf suggested, it seems that trust and kindness still have the power to touch Gollum's heart, for there, just before they enter Shelob's lair, Gollum comes upon the two hobbits sleeping, Sam with Frodo's head in his lap. We are not privy to Gollum's thoughts, but the green glint of malice falls from his eyes. "For a fleeting moment, could one of the sleepers have seen him, they would have thought that they beheld an old weary hobbit, shrunken by the years that had carried him far beyond his time, beyond friends and kin, and the fields and streams of youth, an old starved pitiable thing" (II:382). His touch on Frodo's knee is almost a caress.

But then Sam wakes up and speaks sharply to him, and the moment passes. The green glint returns, and Sméagol's final chance to repent falls away, but without Frodo's compassion it is unlikely he would have had any such chance.

Throughout the psalms, David rejoices that he has not sat in the company of the wicked. Yet Jesus dined with all manner of sinners. Gollum is worse company than even the worst of sinners: simpering, cloying, selfish, devoid of the compassion he craves; moreover, he has nasty eating habits. Yet Frodo is unfailingly kind to him. It is this, more than anything, that proves that Frodo is resisting the evil power of the Ring. He is clinging to his faith, reminding himself of his own weakness and resisting the desire to hate.

XVIII

TRUSTWORTHINESS

RODO IS MORE GUARDED with Faramir, telling him only that he is an enemy of the One Enemy and asking to be left alone. Ever since the incident with Boromir, he has been mistrustful of Men.

In light of the trust he places in Gollum, this may seem odd, but what he knows of Men bears out his logic. Gollum possessed the ring for nearly five hundred years, and yet he did not fade as did all nine of the Ringwraiths, who had begun as mortal Men. Of all the peoples given rings of power, only those of human stock surrendered wholly to evil and to the service of Sauron. To Frodo, Men are as strange as Hobbits would be to us if we were to meet some of them in the woods today. The only Men he's gotten to know are Strider and Boromir (Gandalf may look like a Man, but he is not), and he was mistrustful of Strider at first.

Faramir tells him many fair-sounding things, such as that he wishes only to see the White Tree of Gondor in flower again, the city full of light and beauty and peace, "not a mistress of many slaves, nay, not even a kind mistress of willing slaves" (II:331). War may be necessary, but he claims to love it not, only that which it defends.

Frodo is tempted, upon hearing all this, to unburden his heart to Faramir, but he restrains himself, thinking, "Better mistrust undeserved than rash words" (II:331).

Faramir is someone to whom Gandalf entrusted all his names, even the name he was called by in the West when he was young, Olórin, which is recorded nowhere else in the trilogy (II:329). This in itself should hint to Frodo and Sam that Faramir is worthy of their trust. Nevertheless, they remain wary of him until his obvious respect for Elves causes Sam to warm up to him and drop his guard.

Sam does not have even a tiny fraction of Gandalf's wisdom in his head, but in his heart he is Gandalf's equal—perhaps the only such equal Gandalf has in Middle-earth. At any rate, in the folly of his head and the wisdom of his heart, he reveals to Faramir the identity of Isildur's Bane, and Faramir's trustworthiness is put to the test. Echoing Éomer, he says, "We are truth-speakers, we men of Gondor. We boast seldom, and then perform, or die in the attempt" (II:342). He reassures them that they have nothing to fear from him.

Now that Faramir has proved his mettle, Frodo can no longer dissemble. He tells Faramir that he has been charged with casting the Ring into the fire. "Gandalf said so. I do not think I shall ever get there" (II:343). And at last he collapses from weariness. As they carry Frodo to bed, Sam pays Faramir a compliment. "You took the chance, sir," he says.

"Did I so?" asks Faramir.

"Yes sir, and showed your quality: the very highest" (II:343).

When Faramir asks what he should do with Gollum at the pool, Frodo is faced with a similar choice to the one he faced in the Barrow. With a word he could be free of Gollum forever, but he finds that he can no more countenance Gollum's death than he could allow himself to escape from the Barrow Wight by leaving his friends behind.

Gollum does not respond so well to Frodo's kindness, as he feels betrayed, but Frodo does not on that account regret his choice. He has done the best he could in a difficult situation, and his conscience is clean. It is far more important to *be* trustworthy than to *seem* trustworthy, a lesson he learned from a lanky man named Strider long ago.

Faramir, though he has proven himself completely trustworthy, nevertheless wishes he could take the responsibility of trustworthiness away from Frodo. "It seems less evil to counsel another man to break troth than to do so oneself, especially if one sees a friend bound unwitting to his own harm" (II:355). Faithfulness is a mighty virtue, requiring stern character, but to see others struggling under the weight of it moves us as often to pity as to respect. When we have the opportunity to give counsel to such a one, we may do well to remember Gandalf's admonition that "even the very wise cannot see all ends" (I:85).

Even Gollum desires to be worthy of trust. Both Faramir and

Frodo question him about Cirith Ungol, but he cannot bring himself to tell them that the way is unguarded, though it would make his treachery easier if they believed that. He is divided, and although he has an evil plan, he has not committed himself to following it. He is, perhaps, wishing to be a trustworthy guide in case the Sméagol side of him should win out. He does not want to betray the trust Frodo has put in him, for this is the first time in many centuries that anyone good has trusted him.

Most of us, I'd wager, fall into the category of those with divided loyalties. We want to do good, but we have evil designs. We aren't at all sure they will work, much less whether we truly want them to, and so we try to serve both ends, and both halfheartedly. Jesus said, "No one can serve two masters; for a slave will either hate the one and love the other, or be devoted to the one and despise the other" (Matthew 6:24). But though we despise our sin, we are still devoted to it, and the time of reckoning will come sooner than we think.

Sam, as ever, is the most faithful of friends. In the passage of the Dead Marshes, when all three travelers are feeling the weight of the evil they are approaching, "Sam's mind was occupied mostly with his master, hardly noticing the dark cloud that had fallen on his own heart." His character as a gardener urges him instinctively to tend Frodo like a farmer who braves a hailstorm to cover his plants, barely feeling the peltings on his own back. "He put Frodo in front of him now, and kept a watchful eye on every movement of his, supporting him if he stumbled, and trying to encourage him with clumsy words" (II:281).

When we "look not to [our] own interests, but to the interests of others" (Philippians 2:4), we often find that our struggles are not too difficult to bear. Faithfulness to others ironically makes our own lives easier. This is a difficult truth to put into practice, but it is a rewarding one, whether the object of our faithfulness is a beloved master, like Frodo, or a revolting creature like Gollum who was nonetheless created good. We can see the truth of this in *The Lord of the Rings*, but how will we know its truth extends beyond the Third Age of Middle-earth unless we try it ourselves?

XIX

WISDOM

NE OF THE THINGS the Ring bequeaths is sight. In forging it, Sauron hoped to lay bare the minds of all who wore the other rings, to spy and to pierce the secrets of his enemies. Sauron wishes to be invisible to others and yet able to see all. He is the Eye, lidless and aflame. But without the Ring, he must hide his doings with murk through which not even he can see. Thus he needs the Ring. Yet it is not perfect, for it offsets the wearer half a step into another world, a spiritual realm, from which the physical world looks shadowy and dim.

A part of this power of seeing is bequeathed to Frodo simply by virtue of possessing Sauron's Ring. He is able to see the character and motivation of those he meets more keenly than others. But the vision the Ring gives is not always trustworthy. At times when Frodo feels the Ring is in danger of being taken from him, he sees trusted friends turn into greedy monsters.

True wisdom is the ability to see things as they really are. This is a gift the Ring cannot bequeath. What wisdom Frodo has must come from a different source. But it is interesting that Frodo is quicker to put his trust in Gollum than in Faramir. His sight is keen, but it is directed by a will other than his own, just as the Orthanc-stone is. Very little that he sees gives him hope.

Faramir's discernment is of the merely mortal sort and is therefore not necessarily tainted by evil. Though he is charged to slay any creature he finds in Ithilien who is not there by Gondor's leave, he trusts enough to his own wisdom to hear the hobbits out before he decides what to do with them. He is able to discern much that Frodo leaves unsaid, and when he realizes he is getting too close to subjects that should not be spoken of in the open, he steers the conversation toward lesser matters. In everything he does his wisdom is evident, but even though he meets the hobbits on the very borders of Mordor, Faramir cannot guess to what destination they are toiling. This is a sign of hope, for if Faramir cannot guess, than Sauron must not have the slightest shadow of an inkling of suspicion.

One advantage that good has over evil is that the good who are wise can understand evil, for they accept the evil within themselves, but the evil, in turning away from the good, in rejecting whatever is good within them, come to believe that there is no good, except that which benefits themselves. Assuming themselves nevertheless to be wise, they believe that, if there were any "higher good," they themselves would have seen it long ago and embraced it. Having decided that that higher good does not exist, they become transparent to the good, and yet blind to it, which is a wonderful (for those who oppose him) twist on Sauron's intentions in forging the Ring.

Wisdom is not so much about intelligence, or the ability to strategize, or see all the possibilities. It is about the heart. Faramir tells Sam, "Your heart is shrewd as well as faithful, and saw clearer than your eyes." (II:342) When Sam believes his master lies dead of Shelob's sting, his internal debate is heart-wrenching. His head tells him he must go on alone, that the quest is bigger than his devotion to Frodo. He is too humble to readily believe that that was why Fate chose him to accompany Frodo, yet Frodo appears dead, and the fate of the whole world depends on the Ring's destruction. So he goes against his heart and takes the Ring, and the Phial of Galadriel, and sets off alone into Mordor. It would be a funnier image if it wasn't so heart-breaking. Yet even that mistake is redeemed, for thereby the Ring is kept from the Enemy's hand.

XX

Hope

ROM THE MOMENT Frodo beholds the wasteland that fronts the Black Gate, what little hope he ever had begins to leave him. The decision to brave the gates or follow Gollum to Cirith Ungol seems almost moot. "And if both led to terror and death, what good lay in choice?" (II:297). Fortunately his companion is Sam, whose hope is undiminished. As they watch an army march through the gates, Sam's simple mind sees no cause for despair but rather an opportunity to see an Oliphaunt. His recital of the Oliphaunt poem makes Frodo laugh, "and the laugh . . . released him from hesitation" (II:300).

All living things participate in the struggle to hope. Only before the Morannon, the Black Gate of Mordor, has all life and all hope failed. But as they pass into Ithilien, where "a dishevelled dryad loveliness" yet remains, the spirits of the hobbits lift.

"Gollum coughed and retched; but the hobbits breathed deep, and suddenly Sam laughed, for heart's ease not for jest" (II:305). On their way to the Cross-roads they pass a belt of mighty trees, "still towering high, though their tops were gaunt and broken, as if tempest and lightning-blast had swept across them, but had failed to kill them or to shake their fathomless roots" (II:366). When they reach the Cross-roads, the last bit of sunlight they will see for some time gleams upon the fallen head of the statue of a king and the life that mindlessly reverences it: "A trailing plant with flowers like small white stars had bound itself across the brows as if in reverence for the fallen king, and in the crevices of his stony hair yellow stonecrop gleamed." Frodo responds to this sight with renewed hope, saying, "They cannot conquer forever!" (II:367).

Then they come to the Morgul Vale and witness the vast army that issues from it, and his renewed hope utterly departs from him. "I am too late," he thinks. "All is lost. I tarried on the way. All is lost. Even if my errand is performed, no one will ever know. There will be no one I can tell. It will be in vain" (II:373). In the midst of the mightiest deeds, guilt may steal up to tell us it's not enough, we didn't do everything we could have, we didn't understand how important our task was, and now it's too late.

Overcome with weakness, Frodo falls asleep even as the hosts are still crossing the bridge. Yet when he wakes he finds that "despair had not left him, but the weakness had passed. He even smiled grimly, feeling now as clearly as a moment before he had felt the opposite, that what he had to do, he had to do, if he could, and that whether Faramir or Aragorn or Elrond or Galadriel or Gandalf or anyone else ever knew about it was beside the purpose" (II:374).

Hope is not a feeling, it is a choice; and even in the midst of despair we can still choose to carry on. There is no greater hope than that.

XXI

IMAGINATION

T THE ENTRANCE to the lair of Shelob, Frodo and Sam sit against a wall and imagine what kind of story they're in and how people might hear it in the years to come. This gives them hope and a sense of perspective, and actually makes Frodo laugh, "a long clear laugh from his heart. Such a sound had not been heard in those places since Sauron came to Middle-earth" (II:379). The hobbits have a sense of having an audience and of not being alone. Others have gone before, and others will come after, and the actions we take right now will resonate in both directions, redeeming the sacrifices of those who came before and paving the way for those who come after, maybe making their road just a little bit easier.

A short time later, leaning over Frodo's body, assuming his master is dead, Sam tries to continue to think in terms of the story he is in. Up till now he has been a supporting player, and that is a safe role to play. There is no pressure. There is no loneliness. There is only doing your best by your friend. But now that the friend is gone with the errand still unfinished, Sam finds himself on the very edge of Mordor and there is literally no one else. He could not possibly be more alone. In every other instance when he has felt torn in two (and there have been many), he has always been able to choose to remain by Frodo's side, but now that path has reached a dead end. To die by his side would be "not even to grieve" (II:403). Revenge on Gollum leaps to his mind as a suitable pursuit, but that too would be empty comfort.

Gandalf thought there was a part for Gollum to play, and Sam felt that there was something he himself would have to do before the end. He does nothing at all for as long as he can, then composes Frodo's body, takes Sting and the phial, slips the Ring from Frodo's neck and sets off, telling himself over and over that he has made his decision, though it is "altogether against the grain of his nature" (II:404).

In Mordor there is no hope, and they are on the very border. It is their last chance to give up, and both of them are given the opportunity. It is a temptation far greater than Galadriel's, but it is a true choice. If they do not wish to go, they do not have to. Once they enter Mordor there will be no turning back.

They pass the test. They put the fate of the world above their personal concerns and choose hope even as despair closes over them. Had they been unable to pass this test, they most assuredly would not have been able to continue all the way to the Mountain. Yet they pass the test. There is hope that they will succeed.

Imagination is the whole point of Middle-earth. It's why we

keep coming back. It tells us not so much how to live as how it is possible to live. It reminds us of what's beautiful and important in the world, because for all our technological and societal "improvements," nothing in Middle-earth is gone save the specific people. Humans are all that remain—only the rocks remember the Elves and Dwarves and maybe even Hobbits. But there are still friends, there is still devotion, there are still deeds of renown to be attempted. And they must be attempted if imagination is to be of any value. Idle daydreaming is useless unless it leads to action.

Are there not enough heroes left in the world? Become one yourself. Reject the Ring of Power, the Ring of Doom, leave behind your home, your family, and all but a few of your closest friends, and when you reach the edge of despair, when you realize you were stupid to set out, and your cause is finally revealed to be hopeless, remember Frodo and Sam sitting at the entrance to Shelob's lair, telling each other stories, trying to imagine how their own story would sound being told by a fireside to children. Then grab your stuff and walk into the tunnel, knowing there's likely to be something nasty inside, but trusting that you're part of a story, and what's really important is not whether you succeed or even live through the night, but that you make a good end, one worthy of a story, one that people would want to hear over and over again, even if there's no one to tell your story after you've died a horrible death. Let the angels tell it amongst themselves, and put their hands to their mouths in wonder and amaze.

Part Five

THE GOOD FIGHT

Book V in *The Return of the King*

XXII

SUBMISSION

U PON MEETING THE KINGS OF MEN, both Merry and Pippin feel compelled to pledge fealty in their service. Pippin is partly motivated by pride, ironically enough, though he is also honoring Boromir's memory. Merry is moved by sudden love for the old king. The difference between the two young hobbits mirrors the difference between the two kings. Denethor is full of pride and near to despair, while Théoden is humble and embraces a new hope. Nevertheless, neither hobbit is truly serving the Men but what they represent: glory, honor and stewardship.

Submission is properly a two-way relationship. Théoden and Denethor are under submission as well. Gandalf gains a great ally when he urges Théoden to submit to his role as king, yet loses another when he tries to remind Denethor of the limits of his authority as steward.

Merry and Pippin never include obedience in their submission. They use discernment and their own simplicity to make decisions according to their hearts. So Merry rides to war with Dernhelm against the king's command, and Pippin leaves his post and does what he can to save Faramir. Because they dare to render their service to a higher good than human authority, Merry saves Éowyn, Pippin saves Faramir, and the two might otherwise have died before they met.

Éowyn is a less willing servant than Merry and Pippin, yet her service has been lifelong. She has lived under the same lies as Théoden, and now that they are free of them, she too desires to ride forth into battle. Yet Théodon orders her to govern the people in his absence, and she is constrained by this duty from following her desire. She demands of Aragorn, "May I not now spend my life as I will?"

He answers, "Few may do that with honor" (III:62).

She accuses him of merely putting her in her womanly place, but it is not so. Aragorn will not gainsay the command of another king. Their parting grieves him, but "only those who knew him well and were near to him saw the pain he bore" (III:63).

For many of us submission is a cage, and the decision whether or not to break out of it can be agonizing. In the end Éowyn leaves her people shepherdless and, disguised as a man, rides with the Rohirrim, taking Merry with her. Her motivation is skewed, as her decision is not made in humility but from a desire to win fame. Yet it was foretold long before that the chief of the Ringwraiths would not be killed by the hand of Man, so it seems that she is fated to vanquish him and come to Gondor. Is she right or wrong in her decision? Now we see why the Elves are wary of giving counsel.

Faramir's submission to his father is more devout but no less difficult. Denethor is not unlike Saruman, accusing both Gandalf and Faramir of overarching pride and folly. Yet Faramir never acts on the lies of his father, though doubtless they fester in his heart. He does all things in wisdom and humility, just as Gandalf does, and is renowned among his people for being able to "govern both man and beast" (III:102). For all his father's accusations, he remains governable himself, and though he has already faced the dread of the Nazgûl, he echoes Frodo at the Council of Elrond when he says, "Since you are robbed of Boromir, I will go and do what I can in his stead—if you command it" (III:98)—even if that means facing the Nazgûl again, which of course it does.

Even the servants of Sauron know something of submission and humility. The Lieutenant of the Tower of Barad-dûr who meets the Captains of the West before the gates of Mordor has forgotten his own name, has lost his self, as it were, has become nothing other than the Mouth of Sauron. This is a twisted submission, for servants of the Highest are called to be ever more fully themselves. Yet submission cannot be wholly twisted to evil. In the beginning Sauron himself was a servant. He was cruel and evil in every way, "and was only less evil than his master in that for long he served another and not himself" (*Silmarillion*, p. 26).

Of all the races represented in Middle-earth, it is ever the humans who have the hardest time submitting to the good. Sub-

mission is one of the highest virtues we can attain, but if it were
the only way to achieve good ends, God would not have changed
his mind about destroying all living creatures from the face of the
earth with a flood. None of us are as fully submissive as we ought
to be, yet God will take whatever service we give and make of it
what he will. Thus the glory belongs to him, and there is nothing
in which any of us can boast.

XXIII

STEWARDSHIP

ANDALF TELLS DENETHOR, "But all worthy things that are in peril as the world now stands, those are my care. And for my part, I shall not wholly fail of my task, though Gondor should perish, if anything passes through this night that can still grow fair or bear fruit or flower again in days to come. For I also am a steward. Did you not know?" (III:32).

Legolas and Gimli, as they pass through the streets of Gondor, speak of what their people will do should they be victorious over Sauron. Elves will bring birds and trees and tend the gardens, and Dwarves will bring masons and tend the stones.

Now that Wizards, Elves and Dwarves are gone, the stewardship of all these things falls to us.

Ghân-buri-Ghân is the leader of a band of men who live more simply even than Hobbits. They live like wild animals, and they are keenly attuned to the natural world. Ghân-buri-Ghân knows the time of day even though the murk of Mordor stretches from horizon to horizon, and he senses the shifting of the wind long before the most sensitive of the Rohirrim. These wild men have no desire to go to war, but like the Ents, they have an abiding hatred of Orcs and the havoc they wreak on all that is living and lovely. If there is any good in war, from their point of view, it is that such destruction will come to an end.

When Moses is instructing the Israelites in the rules of warfare, he instructs them not to cut trees down wantonly: "Are trees in the field human beings that they should come under siege from you?" (Deuteronomy 20:19). This is Orc work, and yet it is all too common today. We refer to those things that come from the ground (whether plants, stone or oil) as "resources," but their primary purpose is not to provide us with food, shelter and energy, as good as all these uses can be. They are valuable as they are, aside from whatever uses human beings may put them to.

What authority we have has been given to us. As such, it is limited. Gandalf tells Denethor, "Authority is not given to you, Steward of Gondor, to order the hour of your death" (III:141). Denethor has the title Steward, but he has forgotten, if he ever knew, what his title means. In the end, he looks on despair and fails to laugh. Having lost hope himself, he wishes to spare his son the torture of defeat by killing him before the enemy gets the chance. It is a terrible, twisted kind of caring, and the only good that comes from it is that Faramir is the one to present Aragorn with the crown. Denethor, in his pride, might have contested Aragorn's claim and made all kinds of trouble, but it is unlikely that Aragorn would have wished to avoid such conflicts at the cost of the Steward's life.

Jesus, when healing, sometimes accomplished the miracle by saying, "Your sins are forgiven" (for example, Mark 2:5). For healing is not entirely about physical well-being. The influence of evil is the greatest hurt, as seen when Pippin uses the Palantír or when Merry, Éowyn and Faramir are felled by the Black Breath.

The greatest gift a king can bring his people is healing. King David subdued the land all about so that his son Solomon could have the chance to build the temple and contemplate wisdom. Aragorn, having passed through the Paths of the Dead, comes in victory to Gondor bringing life.

Aragorn uses *athelas* to bring this blessing. *Athelas* has little virtue beyond cleansing fouled airs or easing headaches, but in the hands of the king its fragrance touches the soul and brings healing to mind and body. As we are stewards of the natural world, so can the natural world minister to us, not only through medicinal plants but through beauty, freshness and the simple joy of all life. These things have a measure of power to heal our souls.

XXIV

COURAGE

ATTLE IS THE MILIEU most often associated with courage, but in battle courage is often the only alternative to death. In some ways it takes more courage simply to show up.

Not that I would know. I suppose I've shown courage here and there. I've learned from the shame of early cowardice to stick up for people who are being picked on, even when I end up looking foolish by doing so, even to the person I'm trying to defend. But I've never faced battle or trauma or any kind of real emergency. I've never put myself forward to defend someone in physical danger. So everything I know about courage comes from books and other media.

Reading a good story puts us in the place of the characters. When we are immersed, fully immersed, and one of the characters we are reading about displays great courage, it can seem as if we ourselves are being courageous. One of the best examples is Merry confronting the king of the Nazgûl.

Théoden crying, "Up Eorlingas! Fear no darkness!" The Nazgûl "turning hope to despair, and victory to defeat." Merry "crawling on all fours like a dazed beast." Dernhelm, "faithful beyond fear; and he wept, for he had loved his lord as a father." The laughter that revealed Dernhelm to be Éowyn, and the amazement that caused Merry to open his eyes, after which "pity filled his heart and great wonder, and suddenly the slow-kindled courage of his race awoke. He clenched his hand. She should not die, so fair, so desperate! At least she should not die alone, unaided." The shattered shield, the broken arm, the dual sword-strokes, and the dreadful shriek of the vanquished Ringwraith. It is the greatest deed of any save the Ring-bearers. "And there stood Meriadoc the hobbit in the midst of the slain blinking like an owl in the daylight, for tears blinded him" (III:126-29).

How distant seems the time in Bree when Merry went for a walk and was knocked unconscious by the mere breath of one of these Black Riders. Before that he had been easily snared by the Barrow Wight, and before that he was lulled to sleep by a singing tree. Yet by the time he left the last of the Company behind to follow Théoden, Aragorn could say of him, "He knows not to what end he rides; yet if he knew, he still would go on" (III:57). To face the unknown even while flinching, unsteady or down-right terrified: this is courage.

But courage is not needed only for undertaking perilous tasks. When the winged shadow casts dread upon the people of Gondor,

Pippin and Beregond, sitting on the walls, blanch and contemplate their doom. Then Pippin looks up. The sun is still bright and the wind still strong, and he says, "No, my heart will not yet despair. Gandalf fell and has returned and is with us. We may stand, if only on one leg, or at least be left still upon our knees" (III:41).

Later, as the two are reunited on the wall and the shadow comes again, Beregond says, "Take courage and look! There are fell things below" (III:89). It takes courage even to witness such things without losing hope.

Courage seems to be made up of equal parts pity, wonder, love and faithfulness, occasionally mixed with a liberal dollop of wrath. It is ordinary virtues pushed to extremes. Because of a pity similar to Merry's, Bilbo, Gandalf and Frodo refuse to kill Gollum, having mixed the above virtues with wisdom and mercy. It is love that holds Gimli to the Paths of the Dead, even though he is crawling on all fours as Merry does later. It is faithfulness that keeps Sam forever at Frodo's side, no matter the danger. It is wonder that keeps us glued to the pages.

Wrath is an important facet of courage. Wrath in the good sense is the Ents roused up against Saruman, or Gandalf coming to Faramir's rescue, both on the field and in his father's arms. It is Glorfindel coming against the Nine Riders. I can see it in the story, and I can understand its goodness, but can I ever bring it to bear on the events of my life? I can only hope.

XXV

MIRTH

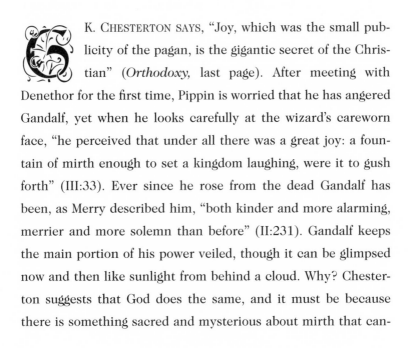K. CHESTERTON SAYS, "Joy, which was the small publicity of the pagan, is the gigantic secret of the Christian" (*Orthodoxy,* last page). After meeting with Denethor for the first time, Pippin is worried that he has angered Gandalf, yet when he looks carefully at the wizard's careworn face, "he perceived that under all there was a great joy: a fountain of mirth enough to set a kingdom laughing, were it to gush forth" (III:33). Ever since he rose from the dead Gandalf has been, as Merry described him, "both kinder and more alarming, merrier and more solemn than before" (II:231). Gandalf keeps the main portion of his power veiled, though it can be glimpsed now and then like sunlight from behind a cloud. Why? Chesterton suggests that God does the same, and it must be because there is something sacred and mysterious about mirth that can-

not be fully experienced in a fallen world.

Even in war there is a kind of mirth, a joy of battle. After Éomer weeps at the sight of his fallen king and sister, his rage is so great that he leads a foray deep into the enemy forces, so far in fact that there seems no hope of return. Just then the black-sailed ships are sighted, and all assume that they contain yet another host of foes. Yet the sight in no way daunts him. He laughs at despair (III:134)—even as Éowyn had laughed in the face of the Nazgûl—and prepares to do such deeds of renown as he assumes will never be remembered.

Then the banner of Elessar is unfurled upon the leading ship, and "the mirth of the Rohirrim was a torrent of laughter and a flashing of swords. . . . And so at length Éomer and Aragorn met in the midst of the battle, and they leaned on their swords and looked on one another and were glad" (III:135).

Laughter eases the heart and has a wonderful power of healing. When Aragorn attends to Merry, he admits to Pippin that the hurt is grievous. "But these evils can be amended, so strong and gay a spirit is in him" (III:159). This is extraordinary, for only a few hours earlier Merry had been wandering lost through the city, unable to keep up with the procession escorting Éowyn and the bier of Théoden. When Pippin finds him at last and tries to lead him to the Houses of Healing, Merry asks, "Are you going to bury me?" (III:148).

The question always makes me set down the book for a moment, bow my head and sob. I can't even write it down without dropping tears into my lap. "But these evils can be amended, so strong and gay a spirit is in him."

Pippin meets even what he believes to be his death with laughter. As he lies crushed by the troll he has slain, his thought "even as it fluttered away . . . laughed a little within him ere it fled, almost gay it seemed to be casting off at last all doubt and care and fear" (III:187). This mirth, this secret joy, is what awaits us in heaven.

The Lord of the Rings is neither a comic nor yet a wholly tragic tale, but it is overflowing with mirth and saturated with loss. "Shall we weep or be glad?" asks Gandalf at the passing of Denethor, Théoden and the winged shadow (III:145). The psalms offer a possible answer. "Weeping may linger for the night, / but joy comes with the morning" (Psalm 30:5). In this world of night, the morning has not yet fully arrived. Evil is grievous, and loss cannot be laughed at, and God shares our grief, and our loss is his own, but his mirth is nonetheless eternal and undiminished.

XXVI

FOOLISHNESS

ROM BEGINNING TO END, this tale is predominantly about the biblical paradox: "But God chose what is foolish in the world to shame the wise; God chose what is weak in the world to shame the strong" (1 Corinthians 1:27). While the truly weak and foolish are waging the real battle, struggling weakly toward Mount Doom, the truly strong and wise do their part by daring to be as weak and foolish as possible, to throw the enemy off his guard. Yet they do not thereby throw off their strength and wisdom. The success of the gambit lies in making the enemy believe that they are strong enough to assail him, or at least that they are foolish enough to believe so. That they would bluff with their very lives is beyond the scope of the enemy's wisdom.

At the brink, "where hope and despair are kin" (III:173), such gambits must be large, daring all and holding nothing back. Éomer, who is neither very wise nor very foolish, admits to not understanding the subtleties of the game but says, "This I know, and it is enough, that as my friend Aragorn succoured me and my people, so I will aid him when he calls" (III:173). Denethor might have called Éomer a fool for being so easily swayed by the mad counsels of Wizards and would-be kings, but Denethor's wisdom has already been shown to be folly. It is only foolishness that is born of hope that can be considered wise.

Is there any such foolishness that the Lord cannot redeem— he who chose fishermen to be his disciples, who rode into Jerusalem on a donkey, who let himself be betrayed by one of his chosen, who thought it would be a good idea to die on a cross in order to destroy death? All of this has been so dwelt upon, so reasoned out, so studied and analyzed, memorized and categorized, that at times it no longer seems strange. But I tell you it's mad, utterly and completely. There is no reason in it, except that it works. Love your enemies? Gandalf says, "As for me, I pity even [Sauron's] slaves" (III:95).

Even having destroyed death, Jesus still does not bring utter peace to the world. Having used foolishness to redeem the world, he has not yet given up on that method. He has the power to wipe every tear from our eyes, but he chooses instead to wait for us to wipe the tears from each other's eyes. And one day, God willing, we will.

Part Six

THE ROAD GOES EVER ON AND ON

Book VI in *The Return of the King*

XXVII

PERSEVERANCE

IN THE END FRODO has no hope of his own left and at times must rely entirely on Sam's. After the long road to Rivendell, after the tragedy of Moria, after the passage of the barren hills, the Dead Marshes, the closed gates and the long way round to the Cross-roads, the stairs, the fight with Shelob, the forced march with the Orcs, the lack of food, water and sunlight, they still have to cross the plains to Mount Doom. Here, some fifty miles from their goal, even Sam's indomitable cheerfulness dies.

But even as hope died within Sam, or seemed to die, it was turned to a new strength. Sam's plain hobbit-face grew stern, almost grim, as the will hardened in him, and he felt through all his limbs a thrill, as if he was turning into some creature of stone and steel, which neither weariness nor despair nor endless barren miles could subdue. (III:234)

By the end of the next day they have covered roughly half the distance, and they are almost out of water. Sam gives a mouthful to Frodo and goes without himself. He cannot sleep for thirst, and at this point he holds his last debate.

Sam is Gollum's complete opposite, and yet they are much the same. They have the same devotion to Frodo, the same indomitable spirit and the same inner dialogue with despair. They have different answers to their inner voices, and that is the essential difference between them—perhaps the only essential difference. Sam hears his own voice tell him, "You are the fool, going on hoping and toiling. You could have lain down and gone to sleep together days ago, if you hadn't been so dogged." His answer: "I'll get there if I leave everything but my bones behind. And I'll carry Mr. Frodo up myself, if it breaks my back and heart, so stop arguing!" (III:240).

At that moment the ground shakes, and a flicker of light from Mount Doom lights the clouds. "The mountain too slept uneasily" (III:241). It seems to me that Sam is vying in perseverance with the mountain. In a world where all things participate in the struggle between good and evil, even leaf and stone, it is as if the evil mountain is beginning to doubt its ability to prevail against a hobbit.

Jesus said, "For truly I tell you, if you have faith the size of a mustard seed, you will say to this mountain, 'Move from here to there,' and it will move; and nothing will be impossible for you" (Matthew 17:20). Although few of us are blessed with Sam's cheerful doggedness, the key to accomplishing such feats as his is simply to keep on believing, to keep on having what little faith we possess.

When the hobbits finally reach the foot of Orodruin, they have still to climb it. It is at this point, pitifully, that Frodo begins to crawl. With Sam the willpower seems almost transparent. He is so other-directed, so focused on the needs of others, that he seems not to need it. He simply does what has to be done. In this case he places Frodo on his back and trudges up the mountain.

Discipline needs to be exercised. It is not a virtue that comes full-formed; it requires focus and attention. In the most desperate ventures, when all hope fails, there is still a choice to be made between stubborn perseverance and the despair that guarantees failure. Only when we stop striving have we truly failed. But to look on despair and yet keep on struggling, that is an awesome thing, and great good may come of it.

On the other hand, perseverance has its dangers. The power of perseverance is seen most clearly in Gollum. In the nearly eighty years since Bilbo took the Ring from him, his single-minded desire has been to get it back again. No fear, no hunger, no reason deters him from his quest, and at the very last he achieves it. That which he had focused all his thought and will on for so many long years is finally in his grasp.

That's the problem, sometimes: anything we want, if we want it hard enough and never stop seeking it, will come to us eventually. That doesn't mean we'll like it when we get it.

The greatest weapon in the struggle to not give up and die is cheerfulness. Sam is much more cheerful than Frodo, and he never stops looking forward. Even at the end of all things, at the

edge of ruin, when the task is impossibly accomplished, he begs
Frodo to move a little farther away from the edge. Out of love for
Sam, Frodo agrees. Even as Mount Doom collapses around them,
Sam says, "'What a tale we've been in, Mr. Frodo, haven't we? I
wish I could hear it told!' . . . But even as he spoke so, to keep
fear away until the very last, his eyes still strayed north, north
into the eye of the wind, to where the sky far off was clear"
(III:254).

And so the Eagles espy them, "two dark figures, forlorn, hand
in hand upon a little hill, while the world shook under them."
They collapse before the Eagles arrive, and do not know that
their hope has been rewarded.

I have little experience with courage, as I mentioned earlier,
but perseverance and I are old friends. I enjoy long drives with
little or no sleep; I have been working on a novel for ten years;
and I love the fact that *The Lord of the Rings* goes on and on and
on. In meeting the deadline for this book I have at times written
for twelve-hour stretches, eschewing food and rest, surviving on
little more than soda and cigarettes. In some small way I have
felt I am walking side by side with Sam and Frodo. But even in
this, my endurance is humbled by theirs. Frodo and Sam persevere not only against the obstacles that stand before them but in
resisting evil. Frodo endures the weight of the Ring and the
temptation to use it. Sam perseveres in mercy, refusing to kill
Gollum even at the end. I am addicted to smoking and have not
developed the willpower to resist it. I know no more of this kind
of perseverance than I do of Merry's courage. My only hope is
that God will persevere in perfecting me.

XXVIII

CELEBRATION

I N ALL THE TRILOGY, in a set of books that brings tears to my eyes throughout, no section makes me sob as heartily as the celebration on the Field of Cormallen. To see Sam, unswervingly faithful servant, be flustered and confused by Strider, all dressed up in king's raiment, kneeling before him, and to imagine his joy and complete satisfaction as the minstrel sings the tale of *Frodo of the Nine Fingers and the Ring of Doom*, overwhelms me with a puissant bliss, and I am fully present in the crowd that witnesses their honor.

And all the host laughed and wept, and in the midst of their merriment and tears the clear voice of the minstrel rose like silver and gold, and all men were hushed. And he sang to them, now in the Elven-tongue, now in the speech of the West, until their hearts, wounded with sweet words, overflowed, and

their joy was like swords, and they passed in thought out to
regions where pain and delight flow together and tears are the
very wine of blessedness. (III:258)

Celebration involves singing and dancing, eating and drinking,
but at its heart it is about remembrance. It is about telling the
old stories, and also the new. It is about praising and worshiping
the Author of those stories.

When Merry asks for a pipe in the Houses of Healing, then
thinks better of it, recalling Théoden's promise to discuss herb-
lore with him, Aragorn urges him to "smoke then, and think of
him!" and thereby honor his memory (III:160). When Sam is in
the middle of Mordor, still far from Mount Doom, he chances to
look up, and through a break in the reek he sees a single star.
"The beauty of it smote his heart . . . and hope returned to him.
For like a shaft, clear and cold, the thought pierced him that in
the end the Shadow was only a small and passing thing: there
was light and high beauty for ever beyond its reach" (III:220). At
its best, celebration is a vision of eternity glimpsed through the
cloud-wrack of our sorrows.

When all things are accomplished and the hobbits begin to
turn their hearts toward home, Aragorn bids them "wait a little
while longer: for the end of the deeds that you have shared in has
not yet come. A day draws near that I have looked for in all the
years of my manhood, and when it comes I would have my
friends beside me" (III:277). If friends are needed in the danger-
ous quest, they are all the more necessary for the celebration.
We may occasionally be able to accomplish perilous deeds alone,
but it is a cold celebration that is lonely.

When the hobbits press Gandalf about the day Aragorn refers to, Gandalf says, "Many folk like to know beforehand what is to be set on the table; but those who have laboured to prepare the feast like to keep their secret; for wonder makes the words of praise louder" (III:277). The secrecy has the same effect as the blindfolds in Lothlórien and Ithilien, shutting off sight for a while so that the beauty of the Naith of Lórien and Henneth Annûn, the Window of the Sunset, should be all the more astounding.

Tonight I saw a star peek through clouds, and I tried to see it with Sam's eyes. But I couldn't. It was just a star, one of the stars I see every night. I live outside Chicago, so I rarely see more than a smattering of stars on the clearest of nights. But when I visit my parents in New Hampshire, I am constantly overawed by the billions of visible stars strewn from horizon to horizon. When I was growing up there I enjoyed looking up at the stars, but their glory was never fully evident to me. Only after spending a good many years elsewhere am I able to apprehend the glory of a heaven unstained by light pollution.

My blindness is not entirely due to overfamiliarity. The glory of that single star is not diminished by my lack of appreciation, but it has been said that "only those who look at the world with pure eyes can experience its beauty" (Josef Pieper, *The Four Cardinal Virtues*, p. 167). Our sojourn through this land of shadow serves to purify our eyes, so that we can fully appreciate the glory and purpose of the final celebration. God's glory is abundant, profuse and extravagant, and "this slight momentary affliction is preparing us for an eternal weight of glory beyond all measure" (2 Corinthians 4:17).

Of course we know what that glorious day will bring: marriage.
The day that Aragorn awaits is his marriage to Arwen, and the
day we all await is the marriage feast of the Lamb, wherein we
will be presented as the Bride. Frodo's words to Gandalf when he
beholds Arwen Evenstar serve as an appropriate response to
both weddings: "At last I understand why we have waited! This is
the ending. Now not day only shall be beloved, but night too shall
be beautiful and blessed and all its fear pass away!" (III:280).

XXIX

JUSTICE

USTICE IS THE VIRTUE of rendering unto others their due. We owe love, worship and obedience to God in the same way that Gollum owes his life to Sam and Frodo, that the people of the West owe honor and gratitude to the same, and that the Steward of Gondor owes allegiance to the King. Justice is also concerned with punishment, vengeance and condemnation, but only those who are innocent can render such judgments. In this world of sin and failure, where "all have sinned and fall short of the glory of God" (Romans 3:23), mercy is our only option.

When the woman caught in adultery is brought before Jesus, he says, "Let anyone among you who is without sin be the first to throw a stone at her." One by one the crowd disperses, until only the woman and Jesus are left. Jesus alone has the right to con-

demn her, since all sin is an offense against God, and he is the
Son of God, perfect and without sin. Nevertheless he says to her,
"Neither do I condemn you. Go your way, and from now on do
not sin again" (John 8:7-11). None of us, neither human being
nor Hobbit, can in good conscience take it upon ourselves to pro-
nounce doom where God has chosen to show mercy.

When Aragorn leads seven thousand to Mordor and some
become faint of heart, he takes pity on them and sets them to a
different task, to lessen their shame. In that dark hour, when he
needs them, he nonetheless will not force anyone to follow him.
The lords of the free wish freedom for all, just as the lords of the
slaves desire slavery for all.

Aragorn continues to choose mercy even when he sits upon
his throne. He forgives the Easterlings who surrender, makes
peace with Harad, and gives to the slaves of Sauron the land
around Lake Núrnen in Mordor. There is no retribution given nor
redress demanded for the damages of the war. Last of all comes
Beregond before the throne, who left his post and shed blood in
the Hallows, for which the penalty in ages past has been death.
Aragorn chooses exile, a doom which causes the blood to drain
from Beregond's face, but it is a just jest, for the King has
appointed him Captain of the Guard for Faramir, for whom he
"risked all, to save him from death" (III:276).

Aragorn is well aware of his own failures and shortcomings, so
that even when he comes into his strength and has proven himself worthy of the throne, he does not forget the grace that set
him there, nor does he fail to extend that grace to all those whom
he would rule.

When Gollum attacks Sam and Frodo as they toil up Mount Doom, Sam has every right to exact his revenge. He has wanted to kill the creature from the moment he laid eyes on it. He has refrained repeatedly at Frodo's request, but now it has openly attacked his master.

The journey to the mountain has changed Sam, purified and transformed him. He is no longer the soft, stupid hobbit who asked Gollum to gather herbs and built a smoking campfire to cook coneys in. Sam is now "a creature of stone and steel" (III:234), and Gollum is no longer any match for him.

Yet instead of fighting or fleeing, Gollum collapses in a heap and begs for mercy. Even as Sam raises his sword, he hesitates. "It would be just to slay this treacherous, murderous creature, just and many times deserved; and also it seemed the only safe thing to do. But deep in his heart there was something that restrained him: he could not strike this thing lying in the dust, forlorn, ruinous, utterly wretched" (III:246). Sam only wore the Ring a short time, but that is enough to offer him a glimpse into Gollum's tortured soul, and that glimpse is enough to stir a pity in his heart that he has heretofore never felt for Gollum.

Jesus says, "Do not judge, and you will not be judged; do not condemn, and you will not be condemned. Forgive, and you will be forgiven; give, and it will be given to you. A good measure, pressed down, shaken together, running over, will be put into your lap; for the measure you give will be the measure you get back" (Luke 6:37-38).

Sam is richly rewarded for choosing mercy over condemnation, not only on the Field of Cormallen but right there on the side of Mount Doom. After Gollum falls into the abyss, Sam beholds his master, "pale and worn, and yet himself again; and in his eyes there was peace now, neither strain of will, nor madness, nor any fear. His burden was taken away." Sam falls to his knees. "In all that ruin of the world for the moment he felt only joy, great joy."

Gollum is gone, but he has played his part, as Gandalf suspected all along. Frodo realizes that "but for him, Sam, I could not have destroyed the Ring. The Quest would have been in vain, even at the bitter end. So let us forgive him!" (III:249-50).

True justice leads to healing, and while none of the hobbits get what they deserve—that is, a happy homecoming to the peaceful land they left behind—Frodo remembers the lessons he learned on the road to Mount Doom and does not turn aside from them when he reaches the wreck of the Shire. Even after Saruman tries to kill him, Frodo commands that he not be slain. "It is useless to meet revenge with revenge. It heals nothing" (III:333).

Saruman responds with "You have robbed my revenge of sweetness, and now I must go hence in bitterness, in debt to your mercy. I hate it and you!" (III:334). Sometimes the mercy we show to the wicked is punishment enough.

Frodo even offers clemency to Wormtongue. When Saruman tries to take that mercy from his servant by describing his misdeeds, Wormtongue kills him and is immediately slain himself. Justice is thereby served, and the hobbits maintain their innocence. As is seen again and again in the story, the wicked, left to their own devices, will eventually kill each other.

As the hobbits watch, a mist gathers about Saruman's body

and rises into the sky. "For a moment it wavered, looking to the West; but out of the West came a cold wind, and it bent away, and with a sigh dissolved into nothing" (III:334). He was given every chance to repent, but he refused, and when his spirit looked toward the West, whence he had come, the West rejected him.

Some injustices cannot be remedied in this Middle-earth. Fingers don't grow back. Nor do friends. The Ring, though he did not ask for it, has corrupted Frodo. He has seen his closest friends take on the appearance of fiends when the Ring came between them. He has been in that misty otherworld of the Ringwraiths. At the final test he chose the Ring for himself alone and refused to cast it into the fire. There is no condemnation possible for this, for the task, by anyone's standards, was too big for him. But a part of Frodo was broken during the long journey to Mordor, and no one and nothing, neither plant nor animal, can restore him to wholeness.

So he leaves. He is given this grace by Arwen, of whom little is told in the main text, except that she has forsaken her kindred and indeed her immortality for love of mortal Aragorn.

Frodo tries to explain his leaving to Sam: "It must often be so, Sam, when things are in danger: some one has to give them up, lose them, so that others can keep them" (III:345). And so Frodo passes out of this world, along with Gandalf and Bilbo, and at last finds the place where his soul can be healed. His maimed finger, I expect, like the wounds of Christ, will remain with him forever as testimony to his deeds.

In that passing Sam Gamgee loses his oldest and dearest

friend. That too is eventually remedied, but it is a bitter fate. Sam has been divided so often during the story, always between Frodo and some other, equally valuable good, from Bill the Pony to the Shire, when he saw in Galadriel's mirror that it might be destroyed. He has loved all good things and wished to protect them at any cost to himself, yet he has ever chosen Frodo above all others.

When Frodo is ready to depart, Sam once more feels "torn in two." Frodo tries to comfort him. "Poor Sam! It will feel like that, I am afraid. But you will be healed. You were meant to be solid and whole, and you will be" (III:342).

XXX

Love

OVE IS THE GOAL and object of every other virtue. It consists, at the most basic level, simply in knowing another person, place or thing, in rejoicing in their existence, in attempting to know them fully and intimately, with no thought of possession but rather of an immersion that borders on self-forgetting. In its highest form, love of other supersedes love of self, and sacrifice thereby becomes possible. *The Lord of the Rings* reverberates with love.

The most obvious love in the tale is that of an Author for his creation. Tolkien takes great care to get to know every character, major and minor, writing entire volumes detailing their lives even when they don't really affect the story of the Ring. The fact that the author knows their stories lends a depth and richness to the parts these characters play that cannot be shortcut by any writerly trick.

Of all the minor characters, Arwen is perhaps the greatest. Her role in the main story is to sit at the feast in Rivendell, weave a banner for Aragorn and arrive at the end of the story to get married. Yet she is older than Aragorn by two and a half millennia, and the tale of her love is tragic, for she has made the same choice as Luthien, from whom Aragorn is descended: renounced her immortality for love of a mortal. The names Beren and Luthien are inscribed on the tombstone Tolkien shares with his wife. As Aragorn dies, he offers her no comfort but says, "In sorrow we must go, but not in despair. Behold! we are not bound for ever to the circles of the world, and beyond them is more than memory. Farewell!" (III:389).

Tolkien's care is not limited to Elves. Even Lobelia Sackville-Baggins, the mean-spirited hobbit who has desired Bag End since before Bilbo left for his adventure with the Dwarves, finds redemption by being one of the few hobbits to stand up to the invading ruffians, attacking the leader with her umbrella. When the hobbits have chased the ruffians out of the Shire, they rescue all those who have been imprisoned.

> Then there was Lobelia. Poor thing, she looked very old and thin when they rescued her from a dark and narrow cell. She insisted on hobbling out on her own feet; and she had such a welcome, and there was such clapping and cheering when she appeared, leaning on Frodo's arm but still clutching her umbrella, that she was quite touched, and drove away in tears. She had never in her life been popular before.

> When she died the following spring, "Frodo was surprised and

much moved: she had left all that remained of her money and of Lotho's for him to use in helping hobbits made homeless by the troubles. So that feud was ended" (III:336).

Many great tales have a major character who is a Christ-figure, someone who exemplifies some aspect of the Savior. *The Lord of the Rings* has many: Tom Bombadil, who breaks down the walls of the Barrow to set the captives free; Gandalf, who dies and rises again; Aragorn, who descends to the dead and emerges as a King with the power to heal; Frodo, who takes sin upon himself and casts it into the fire; and Sam, the servant of all, who carries Frodo on his back when his master's strength is gone.

As a matter of fact, it's hard to pin down exactly who the main character is. Tolkien treats so many of them at various times as though they were central, much in the same way that God treats each of us, at various times, as though his entire story were revolving around ours.

Romantic love, like Gandalf's mirth, is largely veiled in *The Lord of the Rings*. The relationships between Arwen and Aragorn, Rosie and Sam, are largely hidden. Our only glimpse of this aspect of love comes in the courtship of Éowyn and Faramir. After years of living under the influence of Gríma, who desired her but filled her ears with lies, the truths that Faramir speaks to Éowyn, simply his understanding of who she is, transform her. "Then the heart of Éowyn changed, or else at last she understood it. And suddenly her winter passed, and the sun shone on her" (III:271). Love is the ultimate source of healing, and the reason we need to be healed is so that we can learn to love better.

In all its fierceness and fondness, foolishness and freedom, the love between friends is the root and branch that links Middle-earth with highest heaven. It is said that Legolas and Gimli together took the last ship to the Blessed Realm and were the last of the Fellowship of the Ring to leave Middle-earth. There in the West they were reunited with Frodo and Gandalf, Bilbo, Elrond and Galadriel, and Sam, who followed Frodo when Rosie died after sixty-two years of marriage. Merry and Pippin were buried with Aragorn, and so the bonds friendship formed in the course of their Fellowship survived even death. Boromir, who gave his life to save his friends, was borne by the river out to sea.

The main thing we can learn from *The Lord of the Rings* is that we who are in a position to save the world (by which I mean all of us) do so primarily to save our friends.

Conclusion

Reading (or writing) about the virtues of fictional characters has little power to instill those virtues in us. Yet good books can give us a template, a way of understanding the world, so that when our time of testing comes, when the deed is set before us that we alone have been called to do, we will know the choices we face. But as when Sam is defending Frodo from Shelob, when he rushes up to find the enormous spider gloating over his master, he

> did not wait to wonder what was to be done, or whether he was brave, or loyal, or filled with rage. He sprang forward with a yell, and seized his master's sword in his left hand. Then he charged. No onslaught more fierce was ever seen in the savage world of beasts, where some desperate small creature armed with little teeth, alone, will spring upon a tower of horn and hide that stands above its fallen mate. (II:398)

He had been practicing, you see. He *is* both brave and loyal. Had he not been, he would never have dared assail Shelob, and his reaction would have been mere helpless terror instead of rage.

Of course rage alone cannot sustain us when terror is all around us, but there is another power, never named, who can take over for us when we are in way over our heads. Sam had no name for this power, but he puts his hand on the phial of Galadriel, the one solid thing in that horrible place, and calls her name. He remembers the music of the Elves, how they had cried to *"Gilthoniel A Elbereth!"*

And then his tongue was loosed, and his voice cried in a language which he did not know (II:400) a hymn of praise and a prayer of watching over. All we have to do is strive to attain the virtues, so that they feel comfortable within us. When our strength is gone, the Author of Virtues will lend us some of his.

The primary virtue of *The Lord of the Rings* is storytelling. Sam had no more preparation for the struggles and travails he would face than stories: "Of all the legends he had heard in his early years such fragments of tales and half-remembered stories about the Elves as the hobbits knew had always moved him most deeply" (I:69). A gardener who was moved by stories, he lived out a story that moved a mountain.

The only complaint I have with *The Lord of the Rings* (and Tolkien agreed) is that "the book is too short" (I:10). As the ship bearing Gandalf, Bilbo and Frodo passes into the West, I share Sam's sense of loss as the story comes once again to a close, and I take some comfort as well in the silent company of Merry and Pippin as we make our slow way back to the diminished reality we call our home.

I wonder if Tolkien was expressing a fond wish for his own work when he wrote about Merry's blade: "So passed the sword of the Barrow-downs, work of Westernesse. But glad would he have been to know its fate who wrought it slowly long ago in the North-kingdom when the Dúnedain were young, and chief among their foes was the dread realm of Angmar and its sorcerer king" (III:131). The enemies we face today are in many ways the same enemies the world has always faced, and the things we make today, those things that will endure, may someday, long past our own lifetimes, play a part in the grand drama that brings about the Enemy's final destruction. When Gandalf first came to Middle-earth, Círdan the Shipwright gave him Narya, the Red Ring of Fire, to "rekindle hearts to the valour of old in a world that grows chill" (*Silmarillion,* p. 378). That is the gift that Tolkien has given us.

We are written into the Book of Life. It is not a list of names, nor a laundry list of naughty and nice, but a story, one we will someday be able to read in full. There must be a first time for reading it, a time when the ending is uncertain, and that is where we find ourselves now, but one day we may get the chance to read it in full, not just our own part, but everyone's and every-thing's, and maybe we will discover in the pages of that book the true story of Sam and Frodo and their friends. We will have an eternity to read it over and over again, and we will never grow weary of reading it.

Bibliography

Carpenter, Humphrey. *J. R. R. Tolkien: A Biography.* Boston: Houghton Mifflin, 1977.

Chesterton, G. K. *Orthodoxy.* 1908; reprint, Colorado Springs: Harold Shaw/Waterbrook, 1994.

Lewis, C. S. *Perelandra* (1943). In *The Essential C. S. Lewis,* edited by Lyle W. Dorsett. New York: Collier/Macmillan, 1988.

Pieper, Josef. *The Four Cardinal Virtues.* Notre Dame, Ind.: University of Notre Dame Press, 1966.

Tolkien, J. R. R. *The Hobbit.* New York: Ballantine, 1937.

———. *The Lord of the Rings.* New York: Ballantine, 1955.

———. *The Silmarillion.* New York: Ballantine, 1977.

For Reading Groups

For reading group discussion guides on the three books in The Lord of the Rings *(and* The Hobbit *too) visit the title description page for Tolkien's Ordinary Virtues at <www.ivpress.com>. The direct link is <www.gospelcom.net/cgi-ivpress/book.pl/code=2312>.*

Bibliography

Carpenter, Humphrey. *J. R. R. Tolkien: A Biography*. Boston: Houghton Mifflin, 1977.

Chesterton, G. K. *Orthodoxy*. 1908; reprint, Colorado Springs: Harold Shaw/Waterbrook, 1994.

Lewis, C. S. *Perelandra* (1943). In *The Essential C. S. Lewis*, edited by Lyle W. Dorsett. New York: Collier/Macmillan, 1988.

Pieper, Josef. *The Four Cardinal Virtues*. Notre Dame, Ind.: University of Notre Dame Press, 1966.

Tolkien, J. R. R. *The Hobbit*. New York: Ballantine, 1937.

―――. *The Lord of the Rings*. New York: Ballantine, 1955.

―――. *The Silmarillion*. New York: Ballantine, 1977.

For Reading Groups

For reading group discussion guides on the three books in The Lord of the Rings *(and* The Hobbit *too) visit the title description page for* Tolkien's Ordinary Virtues *at <www.ivpress.com>. The direct link is <www.gospelcom.net/cgi-ivpress/book.pl/code=2312>.*